THE USE OF

Animals
IN **Higher**
Education

PROBLEMS,

ONS

Humane Soc
an affiliate of
THE HUMAN
OF THE UNIT

Jonathan Balcombe, Ph.D., has been associate director for education in the Animal Research Issues section of The Humane Society of the United States since 1993. Born in England and raised in New Zealand and Canada, Dr. Balcombe studied biology at York University in Toronto before obtaining his masters of science degree from Carleton University in Ottawa and his Ph.D. in ethology at the University of Tennessee.

Acknowledgments

The author wishes to thank Andrew Rowan, Martin Stephens, Gretchen Yost, Marilyn Balcombe, and Francine Dolins for reviewing and commenting on earlier versions of this monograph. Leslie Adams, Kathleen Conlee, Lori Donley, Adrienne Gleason, Daniel Kossow, and Brandy Richardson helped with various aspects of its research and preparation.

First edition
ISBN 0-9658942-1-5

Printed in the United States of America

Humane Society Press
An affiliate of The Humane Society of the United States
2100 L Street, NW
Washington, DC 20037

Contents

Tables

Foreword

This is a long overdue book. Clearly, concisely, and logically, it sets out the argument against dissecting or otherwise harming animals in our educational institutions, and presents a variety of examples showing that practices of this sort are not only ethically undesirable but also are by no means the best way of teaching children about living systems.

My own study of chimpanzees, which began in 1960 and continues today, has served to blur, increasingly and definitively, the line that used to be seen sharply dividing human from non-human. We are different, we are unique—but we are not as different as we used to think. A true understanding of chimpanzee nature proves convincingly what I learned from my dog, as a child, that we humans are not the only living beings with personalities, not the only beings capable of rational thought, and above all, not the only beings to know emotions like joy and sorrow, fear and despair, and mental as well as physical suffering.

This understanding leads to a new respect for the living beings around us—not only for chimpanzees but also for all the other amazing creatures with whom we human animals share the planet. It is this respect for life that can be undermined in children when they are required to cut up the bodies of dead creatures or harm living creatures, in class. Of course it is wonderful to learn about the amazing complexities of even simple creatures, to learn more about the way they work. But there are many other ways in which children can obtain this knowledge, as described in this book; ways that will not force sensitive and unwilling students to do something they instinctively hate; ways that do not require the repeated use and discarding of dead bodies of creatures killed in order to teach certain aspects of the life sciences. It would seem in such an instance that the teaching is more about death!

Quite apart from the dubious rationale of learning about living things by cutting up their dead bodies, there is a more fundamental ethical issue: would we be morally justified in killing these creatures to learn how they work, even if it was thought to be the best way of teaching children? The use of animals in medical research, pharmaceutical testing, intensive farming, hunting, and so on is widely—and hotly—debated. The use of animals in education is much less often considered, probably because so few people are aware of just how many animals are killed to satisfy demand. Think of the number of dogfish, frogs, and other animals that are required by one biology class and multiply it by the number of classes in all the schools around the world that teach dissection in biology—every year. This gives some idea of the massive slaughter of animals in the name of education.

This type of education subjects the young people of our society to a kind of brainwashing that starts in school and is intensified, in all but a few pioneering colleges and universities, throughout higher science education courses. By and large, students are given the implicit message that it is ethically acceptable to perpetuate, in the name of science, a variety of unpleasant procedures against animals. They are encouraged to suppress any empathy they may feel for their subjects, and persuaded that animal pain and feelings are of a different nature from our own, and that there is little value in animal life.

More and more students are daring to defy the system, to refuse to dissect when this compromises their ethical values. This book documents the law and policy issues surrounding a student's rights to claim a more humane alternative. I well remember meeting Jenifer Graham, who was severely penalized when she refused to dissect in class. The Humane Society of the United States (HSUS) took up her case and, in a precedent setting move, the school was legally required to restore Jenifer's grade in the biology class. That was an exciting day, when a courageous young woman and The HSUS together took a major step towards more humane practices in school.

I hope that this excellent and well researched book will be required reading for all educators and find its way into school and college libraries not only in the United States, but in all parts of the world where schools, in order to teach about living things, are responsible for killing millions of those living things each year. The life sciences should teach children about our relatedness to the rest of the animal kingdom, about the interconnectedness of all life forms on planet Earth. As Albert Schweitzer said, "We need a boundless ethic that includes animals, too." Surely we should do our utmost to help our children move towards a world of compassion and love.

Jane Goodall, Ph.D.
The Jane Goodall Institute
http://www.janegoodall.org
February 2000

Introduction

High school, each desk with a tray on it and a frog, exhaling ether, spread and pinned flat as a doily and slit open, the organs explored and clipped out, the detached heart still gulping slowly like an Adam's apple, no martyr's letters on it, the intestines' messy string. Pickled cat pumped full of plastic, red for the arteries, blue for the veins, at the hospital, the undertaker's. Find the brain of the worm, donate your body to science. Anything we could do to the animals we could do to each other: we practiced on them first.

—Margaret Atwood
Surfacing, 1972

1.1 Scope of This Monograph

The aim of this monograph is to present a comprehensive examination of the issue of animal use in education from an ethical and humane perspective. The monograph seeks to challenge existing notions pertaining to animals in education by drawing widely from the published literature. It covers animal use in middle and high school, in college and graduate education, and in advanced training in medical and veterinary school. The emphasis, however, is on those grades in which animal use is greatest: the secondary and undergraduate levels.

The uses of animals in education range from benign observation of creatures in their natural habitats, to dissection of dead animals, to highly invasive procedures carried out on living animals. The focus of this monograph will be on those methods that incur significant harm or "cost" to the animal, such as loss of life, the infliction of bodily damage, or exposure to physically painful and/or psychologically stressful conditions. These uses all bear moral weight (Rollin 1981), which underlies the intensifying controversy surrounding animal use in education (HSUS 1996).

At the outset it is important to distinguish the use of animals in education from their use in research or testing arenas. For the purposes of this monograph, the use of animals in education refers to the transfer of existing knowledge from one (the teacher or instructor) to another (the student). It is assumed that existing knowledge is not being advanced through this use, although it is acknowledged that what we learn can better enable us to expand human knowledge in the future. This distinction has implications for the importance society may attach to animal use in education.

1.2 Historical Use of Animals in Education

This very brief section mentions significant events leading to the present status of animal use in American schools.

Animals have been used for centuries to train students either through demonstration or through direct practice by the students themselves (Morton 1987). It is not clear when animal dissection first became a regular part of the American high school biology curriculum. Orlans (1993) reports that this occurred in the 1920s, but there are reports of animal dissections being common in U.S. colleges in the late 1800s (Le Duc 1946; Fleming 1952).

Until the 1960s most, if not all, of the contact the average student had with animals in education involved the dissection of dead organisms. Many biology students never saw a living animal (Russell 1996). In the sixties the new Biological Sciences Curriculum Study (BSCS) was introduced by a team of research scientists, science educators, and secondary school teachers under the oversight of the National Science Foundation (National Research Council 1990). BSCS resolved to replace—or at least supplement—the look-dissect-draw-label-memorize approach, with an emphasis on the "hands-on" study of animals.

The positive impact of BSCS was that it encouraged students to actually conduct exercises in scientific inquiry and to think more about scientific and biological concepts. The problem was that it asked students to study life by first destroying it (Russell 1996). Frog pithing,[1] for example, was a major component of BSCS.

As lessons involving the destruction of animals in the classroom increased, so did public concern for these practices. This concern, further stoked by some notorious examples of highly invasive science fair experiments, prompted the National Science Teachers Association (NSTA) and the National Association of Biology Teachers (NABT) in 1981 to adopt a "Code of Practice" for precollege biology. The provisions were clear: "No experimental procedure shall be attempted in mammals, birds, reptiles, amphibians, or fish that shall cause the animal pain or discomfort or that interferes with its health. As a rule of thumb, a student shall only undertake those procedures on vertebrate animals that would be done on humans without pain or hazard to health"(NABT 1981).

Several states, including Massachusetts, New Hampshire, and California, enacted laws embodying the spirit of the NSTA guidelines, and it is ironic that both the NSTA and the NABT have since somewhat weakened their restrictions. For example, in 1985 the NSTA revised its wording to discourage procedures causing "*unnecessary* pain or discomfort" (emphasis added). This gives considerable leeway to permit painful experiments, because what constitutes "necessary" animal use is highly subjective. Many teachers, for instance, believe that invasive experiments on animals are necessary for the preparation of future scientists or medical practitioners (Russell 1996).

In 1987 a California high school student named Jenifer Graham sued her high school for insisting that dissection was the only method it recognized for learning frog anatomy (Lockwood 1989). The case drew substantial, nationwide media attention and set the stage for growing numbers of students to object openly to animal dissection exercises. In the decade since, several states have passed "choice-in-dissection" laws, which affirm a student's right to use alternatives to dissection without penalty.

---

[1] Pithing is usually performed by inserting a sharp probe into the living animal's brain case, often via the nape of the neck, and wiggling the probe vigorously to destroy the brain.

The Quality and Integrity of Science Education

2 CHAPTER

Most of us teach the way we were taught rather than the way we learn.

—David W. Kramer,
winner, Outstanding Biology Teacher Award

2.1 Introduction

How well biology gets taught is an important facet of the dissection debate. This section exposes some of the weaknesses inherent in the traditional animal dissection exercise and examines the oft-cited value of "hands-on" learning as it is applied to dissection. The relevant matter of alternatives and their effectiveness is addressed in chapters 4 and 5 of this monograph.

2.2 Scientific Literacy in America

In its book *Fulfilling the Promise: Biology Education in the Nation's Schools,* the National Research Council (1990) is strongly critical of U.S. high school biology curricula and points to "an emphasis on naming structures" as contributing to the widespread failure of these curricula to adequately teach science (21). A 1988 survey of 12,000 American students found that the mean scores for those who had had a biology course were only slightly higher than those who had not, suggesting that, for most students, biology courses instilled little if any factual knowledge (Beardsley 1992).

It is, of course, impossible to say whether the current emphasis on animal dissection as part of the standard biology curriculum contributes to these findings. But dissection certainly has some pedagogical weaknesses, notwithstanding the teacher's ability. Dissection as usually taught in the schools is weak on both concept learning and problem solving, yet the value of concept-driven teaching in the context of solving problems has been demonstrated (Jacobs and Moore 1998). Generally, dissection is also too focused on the acquisition of facts while failing to teach students to conceptualize and synthesize (Rollin 1981). The memorization of facts and terms is considered "boring" by most students, and most of what is learned is easily forgotten (Orlans 1991). Yet, according to Cole (1990), more new terms are introduced in a typical high school biology text than in the first two years of a foreign language.

An inherent shortcoming of dissection is that it is a destructive (rather than a constructive) process that destroys many of the specimen's structures and their spatial relationships, precluding reexamination by the student (Rosse 1995). Many alternatives, such as computerized dissection simulations, allow the user to reverse and/or repeat the dissection process an unlimited number of times (Richter et al. 1994). The quality and handling properties of preserved tissues and organs also differ considerably from those of freshly killed specimens (Hancock 1995).

The moderately poor showing of American students in International Math and Science Study (IMSS) comparisons (Gibbs and Fox 1999) is doubtless attributable to many causes, but a good deal of the responsibility has to lie with teaching styles and curriculum content. As technological advances in science proliferate in such fields as genetics and biochemistry, there is an increasing need to educate students to grasp relevant concepts. In their new National Science Standards, the National Science Research Council in 1995 listed the following six areas of content for science instruction in the next century:

- cell biology
- molecular genetics
- evolution
- biochemistry
- environmental science
- animal behavior

As Texley (1996) observes, notably absent from this list is comparative vertebrate and invertebrate anatomy. Yet in the American biology curriculum, animal dissection continues to figure more prominently (Beardsley 1992) than in the curricula of many other countries with high student scientific literacy rates. In Sweden and Norway, for example, dissection is rarely practiced prior to the university level (Balcombe, *Animal Use in Education*, in press) and scientific literacy ranked highest in the most recent (1998) IMSS. If dissection occupies too much of the secondary school science curriculum, given the limited amount of classroom time, students may neglect other more important fields and concepts of study (Zierer 1992; Texley 1996). Perhaps there is a need to de-emphasize animal dissection and to redirect students' limited time toward science topics that will have a greater impact on their lives.

2.3 "Hands-on" versus Active Learning

Criticisms of alternatives to dissection include failure to provide a comparable experience because of technological limitations (Schrock 1990; Snyder et al. 1992), the belief that alternatives are not the "real thing" (Schrock 1990; Wheeler 1993), and failure to convey individual variation (Morrison 1992; Wheeler 1993). Each of these criticisms springs from the belief that "you can't replace the real animal" and provides the basis for what is probably the most common defense of dissection—that it is a hands-on learning activity.

The hands-on argument is not conclusive. Hands-on learning is not the exclusive domain of animal dissection. Many hands-on materials and approaches for learning animal biology do not require killing or harming animals. Of materials that mimic dissection specimens, three-dimensional plastic models, while less true-to-life than a preserved animal specimen, allow the user to explore the shape and dimensionality of organ structures (with the added advantages of greater durability, more realistic color, and already labeled parts). Plastination, a chemical process that transforms the tissues of a dead animal into plastic (see, for example, *www.kfuni-graz.ac.at/anawww/plast/pre.html*), yields durable models with equal macroscopic detail to the original. Dissection of owl pellets is a popular activity, and many teachers have their students reconstruct the skeletons of small mammals from these regurgitated artifacts (Bealer 1980). Other models with particular applications to medical and veterinary medical training are discussed in chapter 5.

Even though a learning activity is hands-on, that does not automatically qualify it as the right way to teach or learn. Many hands-on activities could be carried out by students, but for safety, social, or moral reasons they are not; for example, constructing and detonating explosives in chemistry class. Michael (1993) observes that hands-on activities are only effective for learning if the students' heads are being kept as busy as their hands. This point has particular relevance to animal dissection, where the behavior of poorly supervised students can degenerate to a point where little or no meaningful learning is taking place (Hertzfeldt 1994; Solot and Aruke 1997; Long 1997).

Although dissection may aid in the acquisition of manual skill (Wheeler 1993), this fact does not, by itself, necessarily justify killing and dissecting animals. Such skill can more conveniently and more ethically be gained by practicing on nonanimal training apparatus (section 5.4). Some nations recognize the weakness of this justification and have passed laws prohibiting the destruction of animal life merely for the acquisition of manual skill. The Cruelty to Animals Act passed in Britain in 1876 makes it illegal to practice surgery on animals. India's 1960 Prevention of Cruelty to Animals Act (Section 17(2)(f)) states that "as far as possible, experiments are not performed merely for the purpose of acquiring manual skill."

A more meaningful construct for learning with one's hands versus not using one's hands is that of active versus passive learning. Passive learning is epitomized by students sitting in a lecture hall attempting to transcribe what the lecturer is saying, and it says much for the need for educational reform that the lecture format still predominates in the undergraduate learning experience today. Active learning "occurs when students engage additional cognitive processes while confronting the information being acquired (whether visually, orally or tactilely)" (Michael 1993, 37). Active learning is not something that is done for the learners, it is something they do for themselves (ibid.). It involves asking questions, not merely answering them, solving problems, and generating hypotheses. Sampson (1998) calls this "inquiry learning," and it carries the added benefit of learning how to learn, rather than merely learning to become "knowers." Active learning effects better retention, better retrieval, and better application of knowledge to other contexts (Heiman 1987).

One can discriminate between declarative (just the facts) and procedural (problem-solving) knowledge. Facts can be efficiently transmitted by passive learning, but problem-solving skills are learned most effectively by active, hands-on experience.

2.4 Conclusion

It is not known, nor is it easy to know, whether there is any relationship between the use of dissection as a teaching tool and the levels of scientific literacy of students who dissect. Hands-on learning methods are important and necessary, but they are abundantly available beyond dissecting animals. Furthermore, hands-on learning methods are only part of a solid learning environment for science; the learning should also be inquiry based, involving students in both forming hypotheses and solving problems. Animal dissection, as it is usually taught, does not do this, and allusions to the value of dissection as a hands-on exercise are not adequate justification for the destruction of animal life.

2.5 Recommendations

1. Biology teachers should emphasize active, inquiry-based learning, and engage their students in the "doing" of science.

2. Hands-on exercises should be pursued, but not at the expense of animal lives; countless ways exist for achieving exciting, engaging hands-on exercises for students (e.g., having students study themselves or conducting outdoor studies of animals and plants).

3. The time required to perform good-quality dissections should be used instead to make room for more pressing life science topics—such as cell biology, molecular genetics, evolution, biochemistry, environmental science, and animal behavior.

Sociological Issues

Unfortunately, our educational system is programmed to vaccinate us against empathy, against compassion, against working for the common good.

—Leo Bustad

3.1 Introduction

Evidence suggests that people's attitudes toward animals develop prior to adulthood and are fairly constant once formed (Kellert 1985; Takooshian 1988). The extent to which school environments influence the development of student attitudes is not known precisely, but there can be no question that the influence is there and that it may be considerable (Gammage 1982; Solot and Arluke 1997).

When a biology teacher chooses teaching methods that harm animals, what effect might that have on the developing values of the student? Conversely, when a teacher chooses not to harm animals and makes a point of explaining this to his/her students, how might the students be affected? The amount of influence will vary and it is difficult to measure such things, but it is important to consider the implications of how uses of animals in education may be influencing the views of students and the morals of society.

It is the position of The Humane Society of the United States (HSUS) that harming animals in education is detrimental to the development of healthy student values and attitudes toward animals. In fact, as has been argued by St.

Thomas Aquinas and Immanuel Kant, harming animals or being cruel to them may be harmful to society itself, by imparting to students a callous attitude not only toward animals but also, by extension, toward humans.

3.2 Student Feelings and Attitudes

Published surveys show that student concern about the use of animals in dissection and other educational settings is far higher than is borne out by student protest in the classroom (table 3.1). Rowan (1984) and Balcombe (1997b) have noted that student protest takes a great deal of courage in the absence of explicit leads from instructors, and the small number of student conscientious objectors in classes where dissection is used (and hence judged meritorious by the teachers) reflects this. Teachers, especially those who favor dissection, frequently report that conscientious objection to animal dissection among their students is a rare event (e.g., Offner 1995; Freeman 1995; Dudlicek 1998; Schmidt 1999). Based on such reports, Balcombe (1997b) estimates that unsolicited questions about or objections to dissection average about 3 to 5 percent of the class population.

Table 3.1
Published Studies of Attitudes toward Animal Use in Education

Authors	Study Subjects	Principal Findings
Adkins and Lock 1994	28 U.K. high school and college teachers	One in three teachers in charge of biological sciences argued against the use of animals in the classroom, despite such use being extensive among those surveyed.
Arluke and Hafferty 1996	41 U.S. medical students	Moral uneasiness was initially felt towards performing terminal procedures on live dogs, but moral guilt was neutralized by learning absolutions, permitting denial of responsibility and wrongdoing.
Bennett 1994	110 U.S. medical students	78 percent of the surveyed medical students supported a student's right to choose not to participate in required terminal dog labs, and 32 percent felt that, given a choice, they would not participate in such labs.
Bowd 1993	191 Canadian undergraduates	In a retrospective survey, 27 percent of the surveyed students reported having exclusively negative reactions to dissection, and 38 percent reported both negative and positive reactions.
Brown 1989	142 U.S. ninth grade students	50 percent of the students responded that they would choose an alternative to dissection if provided and 90 percent believed that students should be given the choice.
Downie 1989	273 British undergraduates	35 percent of surveyed students in a first year biology course disapproved of dissecting purpose-bred rats, and 50 percent disapproved of infecting rats with tapeworms and killing them to be dissected.

Authors	Study Subjects	Principal Findings
Keith-Spiegel et al. 1993	482 U.S. undergraduates	62 percent of surveyed students felt that it would be unethical for their professor to require them to use electric shock on rats.
Lock 1994	Meta-analysis	Review of comparative studies on dissection practices finds that dissection and vivisection should be discussed in the classroom.
Lord and Moses 1994	200 U.S. undergraduates	56 percent of surveyed students objected to performing live-animal procedures and more than half said they would refuse to participate in the dissection of cats, rabbits, or monkeys if the situation arose.
McKernan 1991	972 U.S. high school students	72 percent of surveyed students felt students should be allowed to use dissection alternatives and 15 to 16 percent reported that they and/or other students asked for alternatives.
Millett and Lock 1992	468 14- and 15-year-old U.K. students	72.5 percent felt that it is wrong to breed animals for dissection, 83.5 percent felt that alternatives to animal experimentation should be found, and 38 percent "would object to any animal material being used for dissection."
Smith 1994	106 Australian schools	34 schools preferred observational/behavioral studies to invasive use of animals, and natural habitats to classroom settings. Over 50 percent reported ethical objections and students nauseated by dissection.
Solot and Arluke 1997	15 U.S. seventh graders	Concluded from responses to fetal pig dissections that the exercise risks fostering callousness towards animals/nature and dissuading students, especially girls, from pursuing careers in scientific fields.
Willis and Besch 1994	144 U.S. medical students	Most surveyed students found dog labs to be helpful; 22 percent felt that this use of animals is morally wrong.

Conversely, teachers who are openly sensitive to student concerns report that many students do not want to dissect animals (e.g., Long 1997; Mayer and Hinton 1990). Asada et al. (1996) found that significantly more students raised concerns about doing classroom experiments on animals if their teachers were also concerned than if teachers had not expressed concerns.[1]

Quantitative studies corroborate this pattern of student concern (see table 3.1). In a retrospective study, 27 percent of Canadian undergraduate college students expressed exclusively negative feelings about the dissections they had performed (Bowd 1993). Nearly half (48 percent) of the undergraduates in Lord and Moses's (1994) survey would refuse to dissect rabbits, and more than half would refuse to dissect cats (56 percent) or monkeys (67 percent). Fifty-six percent also objected to the idea of performing invasive live-animal procedures. In surveys of English high school students, 38 percent would object to the dissection of any animal material (Millett and Lock 1992), and between 33 percent and 50 percent would object to purpose-bred rats being killed for dissection (Downie 1989). Fifty percent of the American high school students in Brown's (1989) study said they would choose an alternative to dissection if it were offered. Among medical students, Bennett (1994) found that 32 percent would not do terminal dog labs if given a choice, and Willis and Besch (1994) found that 22 percent felt dog labs were immoral.

Why is there such a large disparity between the proportion of students who have negative feelings toward classroom exercises harmful to animals (30 to 70 percent) and the proportion who express their concerns to an instructor? A number of sociological pressures may be keeping students quiet.

Obedience to authority, a well-established psychosocial phenomenon (Milgram 1974), is probably a major factor. Students commonly report being pressured by the teacher to dissect (e.g., Carpenter 1992). (Studies showing high proportions of students with negative feelings about dissection are mostly based on anonymous surveys where the student is not accountable to his/her teacher.) Related factors that might keep students silent include peer pressure (Gilmore 1991b; Solot 1995; Balcombe 1997b), fear of ridicule and humiliation (Heim 1981; Pina 1993; Solot 1995; Balcombe 1997b), and fear of receiving a lower grade (Balcombe 1997b). Parental endorsement may also persuade some students to participate reluctantly in an undesirable classroom dissection exercise. Solot (1995) found that dissection received nearly universal endorsement from parents in her study and that this endorsement sent students messages about the importance of dissection.

Solot and Arluke (1997) provide a representative scenario of the pressure that can be placed on students who desire not to participate in classroom dissections:

> The teacher allowed students to not participate if they continued to object and wrote a letter explaining why they were "opting out" of the activity. If they did this, they were given assignments to do from a textbook about the human body while they sat in the hall outside her classroom. The choice not to dissect was presented as only marginally acceptable; the teacher did not explicitly announce the option and students needed to express it repeatedly and emphatically to reach the point where they were allowed even to submit a formal petition—the letter—asking not to dissect. The alternative activity, textbook work, was certainly a less interesting learning experience, and it was carried out in the hallway, not a site where "real" learning took place in the school. (40-41)

Pressure to participate has also been reported in medical schools. Kelly (1991) reported that in twenty-two U.S. medical schools, refusal to attend live-animal labs hinders an individual's chances for admission or promotion through the school's program, even though these labs are not mandatory. In a related example, a student at Boston University Medical School attended an optional rabbit vivisection lab because he saw professors become hostile to students who asked what the alternatives were (McNaught 1998).

It is worth noting that teachers may also face pressure to maintain animal laboratories. A biology lecturer at Illinois Wesleyan University believes his contract was not renewed because he included discussion of the ethics of animal use in his lectures to his students (*Cincinnati Enquirer*, 28 January, 1983—see Rowan 1984). In many cases, biology teachers are not merely encouraged but expected to use animal dissection in their classrooms, regardless of the teacher's personal preference for teaching method (Sam Davis, personal communication, 10 April, 1999–Davis is a biology teacher at Christopher Columbus High School in New York). Teachers are also naturally inclined to employ methods with which they are taught, and there is a case to be made for de-emphasizing dissection and including the use of humane alternatives during the training of biology teachers.

All of these findings underscore the influence that teachers' values and their teaching methods have on students' attitudes and preferences. If a role of the educator is to stimulate critical thinking and not to indoctrinate, these findings suggest that teachers would do well to give students a choice whether or not to take part in a laboratory that they may find distasteful (Rowan et al. 1995).

Qualitative Studies

Most examinations of student feelings about animals in education have been based on quantitative attitude surveys (see table 3.1) that suffer from superficiality. Few qualitative studies of the impact of dissection on students exist. Two recent U.S. student theses may be the first such studies, and they offer considerable insight into the ways students perceive and respond to traditional classroom animal dissection exercises as well as the influences of demographics and the classroom environment.

For her undergraduate thesis at Brown University, Dorian Solot spent several weeks observing and interviewing students in a seventh grade class at a private school in Rhode Island (Solot 1995; Solot and Arluke 1997). She observed the dissections of fetal pigs by two separate classes from start to finish, interviewing fifteen students in all (eight girls and seven boys, aged twelve or thirteen years). Solot also supplemented her study with her own memories of dissection, which she recalled as being remarkably similar to what she observed, and with informal discussions she had with three parents and five teachers or administrators affiliated with three schools.

Consistent with the findings reported from student surveys (see table 3.1), "virtually all of the students felt at least somewhat negative, hesitant, uncomfortable, or ambivalent toward the prospect of dissecting" (Solot and Arluke 1997, 31). The students expressed concern for the origin of the animals they were dissecting. A number of them raised the question to their teacher in the days before the dissection, and nearly half spontaneously mentioned the pigs' origins during the interviews.

One student who approached her teacher about this was told that the mother pig "died of natural causes" while she was pregnant[2]. This response is untrue, and it reflects ignorance, a lie, or the disingenuous suggestion that for pigs in the meat industry, slaughter is a "natural" cause of death. Regardless, it was important to many students that their specimens were unborn and "already dead when you got 'em," as one student said, and the teacher did what she could to minimize the connection between the dissection and the killing of an animal (Solot and Arluke 1997).

One of the boys in the class Solot studied expressed his surprise at how few students looked forward to dissecting as much as he did and acknowledged that a number of classmates almost opted out: "Some people weren't that comfortable with it but they did it . . . . There were a lot of people who really didn't like it but they did it" (44). One of the teachers Solot interviewed discussed her perception that boys would be more subject to peer criticism if they objected and thus less likely to vocalize their concerns. This reluctance carried over into the dissections themselves. Solot (1995) observed that, in more than half the cases, one partner did all the specimen touching and the other either watched or looked away.

As students finished up, they became more likely to play with the specimens' bodies and organs. Boys carried organs around the room with them to show them off to other boys and "gross out" the girls. One boy whistled a death march as he carried his mutilated pig to the garbage can, dissection tools plunged through its head and body like the victim in a gruesome stabbing. A boy and girl in another class were repeatedly denied permission from their teacher to cut off their specimens' heads; both did so anyway at the end of the dissection, proudly parading the decapitated heads around the room (Solot and Arluke 1997).

The students used a number of strategies to cope with their feelings about the fetal pig dissections. The authors report that these were modeled on the context provided by their elders and their society (e.g., teachers, older students, parents, the mass media), namely, that fetal pigs are regarded as mere specimens and that one should not feel ethically or emotionally uneasy toward them (Solot and Arluke 1997).

In her study of seventeen high school students enrolled in an elective biology course at a rural North Carolina high school, Gracia Barr (Barr and Herzog in press) observed students dissecting fetal pigs, interviewed them, and gave them questionnaires about the experience. Nine of the students wanted to pursue careers in science or a medical field. All enrollees had already dissected earthworms, crayfish, clams, and frogs during the course, and alternatives to dissection were not offered to the students. The pig dissection comprised a significant portion of the course, spanning several class periods. Though the teacher occasionally expressed sympathy for the animals, there was little discussion of the ethics of animal use in the course.

The students in Barr's study were unambiguous in their approval or disapproval of the pig dissection. Twelve of the students (71 percent) liked the experience; the remaining five (29 percent) disliked it. Eleven students had no moral objection to dissecting a fetal pig, which was described by the teacher as a byproduct of the slaughter of pigs for food. Three students thought that dissection was unethical (including one of the students who liked the experience), and three were undecided. Despite the overall approval for the dissection, nearly all students (at least fifteen of the seventeen) were reported as feeling at least some degree of sympathy for the animals.

Many of the students in Barr's study felt their confidence boosted by the dissection and felt more convinced that they were cut out for a medical career or other hands-on work with living organisms. None reported that they were turned away from science careers, a finding that Barr regards as not surprising since students extremely averse to dissection would simply not take this elective course.

However, none of Barr's students felt that the pig dissection changed the way they regarded animals, and she found that even the most thoughtful and articulate ones had poorly developed ideas about broader philosophical issues such as the nature of living things and humans' relationship with other animals. Almost none of the students reported that dissection had stimulated their curiosity about such issues.

The findings by Solot and Barr are instructive. Solot's students were several years younger and their course was not an elective, so their greater misgivings towards the exercise is not surprising. Solot's students were also a random sample, whereas many of Barr's students were headed for science or medical careers. That Barr's students lived in a rural setting, where communities tend to view animals in a more utilitarian manner (Kellert 1996), may also contribute to the difference in the findings.

Barr reports that the students in her study had not found the frogs, worms, clams, and fish dissections especially interesting, but that the interest level increased with a mammal (fetal pig), presumably because of the pig's anatomical similarities to humans. Students may leave some dissections in awe of the complexity of living structures and interested in dissecting more of them. But does this awe foster a new level of respect for nature, as some dissection proponents have suggested? Students with animal dissection experience may express interest in dissecting more animals, but this observation provides no evidence about how much they respect animals or life (Solot 1995).

Squeamishness

"Squeamishness" is defined in *Webster's New Collegiate Dictionary* (1986) as being "easily nauseated." It is a feeling commonly associated with animal dissection and was reported by Solot and Arluke (1997) as the most common problem for the students in their study. However, it should be remembered that the students in Solot's study were mostly pre-adolescent; with older students, squeamishness is not usually the basis of student conscientious objection (Balcombe 1997b). An example is Downie and Meadows's (1995) study of students at a British university, where the dominant basis for the more than 300 students who opted for an alternative to animal dissection was objection to the killing of animals for educational use.

Squeamishness is usually perceived as a weakness, and it is also often seen as an inappropriate reason for a student to be excused from a dissection exercise (e.g., Snyder et al. 1992). But Sapontzis (1995) notes that such labels as "squeamishness" or "sentimentality" have been used to demean nonobjective thoughts associated with the animals, including feelings of revulsion or compassion. Perhaps squeamishness should be taken more seriously as a natural product of empathy for others. As Solot (1995) points out, those who call attention to squeamishness as a signal alerting us to the possibility of a problematic activity raise a point that should not be overlooked.

Desensitization

A prominent concern of dissection opponents is that exercises harmful to animals may tend to desensitize certain individuals, making them more callous toward animals and, by extension, toward other humans (Russell 1972; Kelly 1986; Morton 1987; Langley 1989; Gilmore 1991a). For Heim (1981), the desensitized person is either unaware of the animal's suffering, does not care about it, denies its existence, or believes that such suffering is warranted by the importance of the work. Heim (1981) cleverly characterizes desensitization in this context as "diminution by familiarity"(44). In Rowan's (1984) words, "Problems appear when the cult of objectivity leads to the disregard or devaluing of normal sensitivities." Solot and Arluke (1997) conclude from their study of high school fetal pig dissections that the activity risks imparting to students a callous attitude toward animals, nature, and the natural world.

Mayer (1982) describes a contradiction in science education of (1) trying to instill ethical values of caring and respect and (2) trying to instill scientific attitudes of rationality and objectivity. Australian teacher William Smith (1990) notes the difficulty he has encountered in overriding the "'cuddly-furry' response" in seventh grade students. Too often, our use of animals in education reinforces a simplistic view that any manipulation of animals constitutes "science." As Rowan (1984) points out, the unfortunate corollary of this is that any expression of concern for the animal is viewed as sentimental and unscientific.

Miriam Rothschild (1986) made the poignant observation that "just as we have to depersonalize human opponents in wartime in order to kill them with indifference, so we have to create a void between ourselves and the animals on which we inflict pain and misery for profit." In her study of fetal pig dissection, Solot (1995) observed that some teachers attempted to remove the pig from the animal category altogether. Solot also notes the hypocrisy that the animals slaughtered daily to feed Americans will never see the collective outpouring of sympathy and resources that saved the lives of three individually identified whales trapped in Arctic ice in 1988. As one bumper sticker reads, "Why do you love some animals called pets and eat other animals called meat?"

Might these mixed messages create confusion for students trying to develop a cogent set of values toward life? The confusion would appear to have profoundly different effects on different students; some students may come to oppose all animal experimentation, while some others may turn off all moral concern and develop extreme indifference (Heim 1981; Nab 1989). Many students fit one of these two categories of attitude toward other life. The majority, of course, fall somewhere in the middle.

One indication that some students may become desensitized toward animals by dissection exercises is the inappropriate (though perhaps not abnormal) behavior of some students toward the dissected specimens themselves. Mutilation of dissected animals is very common (Berman 1984; Goldfinger 1993; Pendleton 1993; Pina 1993; Long 1997). When students mutilate their dissection specimens, the behavior tends to show a progression from initial apprehension, to confidence, then finally to mutilation.

Solot's study was illustrative of this. Even though squeamishness was common among the students of Solot's (1995) study, students became increasingly immune to such feelings. At the beginning of the dissections, students made jokes like moving a pig's legs to make it walk or dance, and there was a lot of uncomfortable giggling. By the end, however, some were deliberately mutilating and dismembering their specimens, some did crude explorations, such as pushing the animal's organs into its mouth, and some boys were said to have races to see who could "dig out" their pig's eyeball fastest (Solot 1995; Solot and Arluke 1997). At another middle school, a science department head removed dissection from the curriculum when she noticed that students' demeanor toward the animals was no different than if they had been "playing with clay" (Solot 1995).

Researchers have found that students tend to gain an affinity toward whatever learning methods they are exposed to. Lock and Millet (1991) found that students' attitudes toward dissection and animal research were reinforced by participation in or exposure to these endeavors. Strauss and Kinzie (1994) found that high school students' opinion of frog dissection improved when they dissected frogs, while the opinion of students who used an alternative to the dissection improved towards the alternative. Veterinary students exposed to either survival surgeries or to terminal surgeries on dogs tended to support the method with which they had experience (Bauer et al. 1992a). Arluke and Hafferty (1996) documented initial moral uneasiness of medical students towards performing terminal procedures on live dogs and that moral guilt was neutralized by learning absolutions that permitted complete denial of responsibility and wrongdoing. When interpreting studies of student preferences for learning methods, however, it cannot be assumed that preferred methods are also better methods. A recent study reported that U.S. medical students scored significantly higher on questions from computer laboratories than from either didactic lectures or computer-assisted lectures, even though the students perceived didactic lectures to be the best learning method (Richardson 1997).

3.3 Teacher Influence

Without question, teachers can exert an enormous influence over their students. The amount of wakeful time the average North American child spends in the presence of a teacher is not much less than that spent in the presence of his/her parents and, in many cases, may be more. A teacher is every bit as much an authority figure as is a parent, and teacher attitudes, values, and personal preferences are apt to influence those of the student.

There is no escaping the fact that science education, like science itself, is value laden rather than value free, and it involves the absorption not only of facts but also of attitudes (Morley 1978). There is also evidence that the attitudes of those around one may exert more influence on one's attitudes and values than does information and knowledge. The human dimension of the student/instructor relationship can convey values, attitudes, and signals that transcend the content of textbooks and other written curriculum materials (Brennan 1997). Thus, even where a syllabus may be sensitive to the welfare and ethics of animal treatment, a teacher who is indifferent towards these issues will communicate this in both subtle and not so subtle ways (ibid.). Evidence further suggests that neither scientific literacy (Takooshian 1988) nor faith in science (Pifer et al. 1994) is a predictor of attitude toward animal use, and that this pattern applies to children as well as adults (Lien 1993).

In his examination of attitudes of elementary schoolchildren in Newfoundland, Lien (1993) made some intriguing observations. The main influence on whether or not children decided to write letters to their governments to protest seal hunts was not their knowledge of the hunts, but the degree to which they admired the adult who inspired or urged them to write the letters. Lien also found that the original attitudes of the children were usually deepened and expressed more decisively as their knowledge increased. A curriculum module on whales, which demonstrably increased children's knowledge of these animals but did not indicate that there was a right or wrong way to view them, resulted in children from fishing communities becoming more utilitarian in their view of whales and mainland children becoming more protective of them. These findings suggest that information and attitude learning are quite independent. Lien (1993) speculated, probably correctly, that learning is constrained by such factors as the need to fit into a group, and that attitudes are relatively more affected by the attitudes and prestige of the educator than by curriculum content.

The above findings indicate that teachers' influence on students extends well beyond the information that they teach. The classroom is a place well suited to the cultural transmission of values, and teachers may have a substantial influence on the developing attitudes and values of their students.

Many examples exist of teachers using their influence to try to impress their own values and attitudes on students. Rollin (1981) provides the following anecdote: an instructor confronted his psychology student and told him that he might be "soft" and not "cut out for psychology" when the student expressed his horror at the instructor's killing a rat by bashing the animal's head against a wooden desk. An essay by William Jordan (1991) gives a graphic and disturbing memoir of institutionalized animal mutilation from his biology class of 1964 and warns of the cost to humanity and human decency that may accrue. Some science teachers even admit that one of their aims is to desensitize students.

From time to time, teachers step beyond the bounds of what the law allows, and a brief media flurry results. One recent case involved a high school principal taking a small group of science students into his garage, where they killed and dissected cats (*Martinsville Reporter* 1996). In another case, two Indiana high school students shot a puppy and took it to class to dissect after the teacher had instructed them to bring in a specimen of their own. The killing of animals was banned at a school in Wyoming after biology teachers slaughtered pigs on the school grounds (*USA Today* 1996). At an Ohio school, a biology teacher was charged with cruelty for killing piglets by bludgeoning them at his farm (one of his male students then bashed a still-living piglet against the pavement in the school parking lot after the teacher brought piglets to the school) (Nolte 1999).

One of the more subtle ways teachers influence students is by the teaching methods they choose. These methods can carry important messages about values and attitudes. The author of this monograph vividly recalls the instructor of his undergraduate genetics labs demonstrating the preparation of a meiosis lab to the class by taking a large adult male locust and methodically snipping off each of his six legs, then each wing, before finally severing the fully alive insect's head. The impression left by this incident was that the instructor wanted to reinforce the objectivity he apparently felt was required of a good scientist.

It seems a fair conclusion, then, that teaching methods that harm animals can play an important role in formulating and reinforcing a dominionistic view (Kellert 1989) toward animals. As Shapiro (1992) has observed, dissection "is a clear instance of teaching that human interests take priority over those of nonhuman animals, and that science takes priority over nature."

3.4 Alienation from Science

Asociological concern that has drawn the attention of some critics is that the dissection exercise may skew the personality traits (for better or worse) of students who are interested in pursuing careers in the life sciences. Keiser and Hamm (1991) argue that when dissection is not part of the curriculum, students may miss the opportunity to prepare for vocations and become valuable contributors in medicine and other health-related professions. The irony of this assertion is that many students aver that they switched career plans away from the life sciences when they learned that they were required to dissect animals (Orlans 1988b). As Brennan observes, "being forced to witness dissection . . . is a powerful disincentive for some people who would otherwise be interested in biological study" (Brennan 1997, 80). An unfortunate result is that invasive classroom exercises may weed out more compassionate students and select for those less sensitive toward others (Russell 1972, 1987; Finch 1988). The ramifications are evident when one reflects that compassion and caring for others are desirable traits in such professions as medicine, veterinary medicine, and nursing.

Typically, the death of a dissected animal precedes its arrival in the classroom. However, when live animals are used in invasive course exercises, the potential to disturb and traumatize students increases. A student at a large state university (the University of Georgia) had this to say of a frog-pithing exercise: "It was the most unrespectful [sic], tormenting experience of my life. I spent almost half an hour in the bathroom crying." Another student from the same class commented, "Sometimes I wonder, after taking science for the last three and a half years, if this school wants us to learn something or if they just want to know if we have the stomach to kill."

Are there students who actually abandon aspirations of becoming doctors or veterinarians because of disillusionment with what they perceive as callous treatment of animals in education? The available data, while anecdotal, clearly indicate that there are (Orlans 1988b). Pat Davis, who has operated the NAVS (National Anti–Vivisection Society) Dissection Hotline since its inception in 1989, estimates that she has spoken with over a hundred callers who have either changed career goals or avoided biology studies entirely because of dissection assignments (Davis, personal communication, 3 December 1998). Hepner (1994) published statements from several student conscientious objectors to animal dissections in school; several of them changed career tracks away from the life sciences because of the dissections. Finch (1988) describes her own shift away from a career in science, marked by the occasion of frog dissections in her high school biology class. London University zoology student Stephanie Johnson (n.d.) reported that "one student in my year decided to give up zoology after the first year and change to botany simply because she couldn't face the pressure she thought would be put upon her to dissect." Krause (1980) recounts that his daughter avoided zoology classes (and became a vegetarian) after her teacher killed and dissected a fish he brought to class. Jill Kimmel, a biology teacher in Valparaiso, Indiana, almost switched careers away from biology because of her objections to dissection (Krause 1994).

Although dissection assignments undeniably turn some students away from the life sciences, the influence that life science curricula might have on attitudes toward animals is not straightforward. In a study of personality differences between pro- and antivivisectionists, Broida et al. (1993) found that students majoring in fields in which they will be more likely to encounter animal experiments (e.g., psychology, biology, premedicine, and preveterinary science) were more opposed to animal experimentation than were students declaring other majors. The authors give two possible interpretations for this unexpected finding: (1) that opposition to animal experimentation might not steer people away from fields in which they are likely to encounter it, or (2) that students enrolling in such majors are relatively naive, and that exposure to animal experimentation may tend to make them oppose it (ibid.). The authors concluded that their sample of students was not adequate to distinguish between these possible explanations or others.

3.5 Teaching to Care

One of the most important criticisms one can levy at our present science education system is that it does not help to prepare young people to grow up to be caring, feeling individuals. Dissection is rarely broached as an ethical issue by teachers who employ it, despite the benefits of doing so (Orlans 1993; Downie and Meadows 1995). Sieber (1986) found that American biology students were keen to debate bioethical issues, but that their teachers were not. Schrock (1990), an outspoken dissection advocate, discourages teachers from getting into philosophical debates with their students. Bentley (1991), in her vitriolic review of NABT's "insidiously evil publication" *The Responsible Use of Animals in Biology Classrooms—Including Alternatives to Dissection,* decries the inclusion of a chapter titled "Ethical Considerations," which encourages middle and high school students to reflect on ethical problems in science. When it comes to resolving such problems, Bentley is "far from convinced that a seventh grade child can do it better" than professional ethicists. Therefore, she concludes, children should not be thinking about it at all. Berman (1984, 49) states that "we cannot really expect our students . . . to become misty-eyed over a rat."

But the value of including ethical discussions and encouraging critical thinking among students is widely supported (National Research Council [NRC] 1990; Rowan and Weer 1993; Downie 1993; Rowan et al. 1995; Petto and Russell 1999). The NRC (1990) has recognized the need for biology curricula to "foster respect for the environment and for the need to sustain a biosphere favorable for the survival of life"(19). Of 1,610 responses to a survey sent to schools in Australia, Japan, and New Zealand, 90 percent of the respondents thought bioethics needed to be taught (Asada et al. 1996). A survey of 47 biology students at Glasgow University showed that students regard bioethics education as very important to prospective biologists in all branches of study (Downie 1993).

That students often show a poorly developed ethical framework reinforces the need to include ethics in the school curriculum. Values education is an important field that needs attention for a civil society. There is a common failure across the entire education system to teach important concepts and values that transcend the immediate academic field—what Daniel Goleman (1997) refers to as "emotional intelligence." Few people can say that they were taught nonviolent conflict resolution. (Surely the history lessons, in which we study who went to war with whom, don't qualify.) And few can claim to have taken a course whose goal was to help them understand their feelings, or how to nurture strong, loving relationships with others. Hendricks and Hendricks (1992) illustrate the problem well:

> In the realm of emotions, many people are functioning at a kindergarten level. . . . In your formal education, how many courses did you take in dealing with feelings? Personally, we cannot remember one minute spent on learning about these key issues in school, whereas hours were spent on memorizing the geography of South America. It is incredible that we have such a societal blind spot. No one ever landed in jail or a mental hospital because of a difficulty with geography, but both institutions are packed with people who have difficulty with their emotions.

The emotionless way in which animals are encouraged to be used in education is part of this unfortunate legacy. And one of the gravest concerns about harming animals in education is the effect it might have on student attitudes about life in general. As Joseph Wood Krutch (1956) observed: "[The current method for teaching biology] not only fails to promote reverence for life, but encourages the tendency to blaspheme it. Instead of increasing empathy it destroys it. Instead of enlarging our sympathy it hardens the heart."

As early as 1895, animal vivisection was prohibited in some schools on the grounds that it hardened the hearts of the young (Buettinger 1997). According to Buettinger (ibid.), no message had greater prominence in the antivivisection literature of the 1890s than the injury to youth as a result of their observing demonstrations of live-animal experimentation.

The connection between cruelty to animals and cruelty to human beings (including child abuse, spousal abuse, sexual abuse, and murder) has been documented (Lockwood and Ascione 1998), and it is increasingly acknowledged that violent criminals are not inclined to discriminate their victims on the basis of the number of legs they possess. However, there is no evidence that harming animals in a classroom has any negative social consequences. Indeed, there has been no attempt to garner such evidence, and it would be difficult to design a study to explore this possible relationship. Nonetheless, when the practice of classroom dissection was banned in 1998 in the state of Rajasthan, India, the principal argument put forward by proponents of the ban was concern over the potential repercussions of violent teaching methods on young minds (Abdi 1998).

There is, of course, great value in student exposure to animals, either in the natural setting or, if suitable, in carefully researched and devised captive situations (HSUS 1993). Such exposure helps students learn to appreciate the real animal and its experience of life, and to value animals as entities in themselves worthy of ethical consideration and not only as a means to an end (Petto and Russell 1999). Many biology classes today are providing no such learning environment.

3.6 Recommendations

1. Teacher training should be reformed to include exposure to dissection alternatives, and dissection of animals should not be a prerequisite for obtaining a science teaching license.

2. Students should be fully involved in ethical decision making in the classroom.

3. Conscientious objection should not be seen as a challenge to a teacher's authority but rather respected as evidence of concern and reflection.

4. Concern for animals should not be labeled as "squeamishness" but should be acknowledged as a legitimate manifestation of empathy for others. "Squeamish" students ought not be pressured or humiliated into participation in exercises they find distasteful.

5. Teachers and students should be made more aware of the connection between animal cruelty and interpersonal violence; though mutilation of dissected specimens may only reflect a temporary desensitization, it should not be ignored or regarded as an excusable youthful indiscretion.

6. Ethics should be part of the education of all children, and dissections should not be conducted in the absence of ethical discussion about the origins of the animals and the moral implications of using them.

---

[1]When the author of this monograph shared his ethical concerns about a required fetal pig dissection with his students enrolled in a large freshman undergraduate biology course, a disproportionate number of them (12 out of 40, compared with reportedly 3 out of some 700 students enrolled in the rest of the class) elected not to dissect a pig, even though this option required a written statement of justification and a private meeting with course administrators.

[2]Unlike the students in Solot's study, who seemed to carry on fairly obliviously to her presence, Solot noted that the teacher acted suspicious of her, her topic of study, and her presence in the school during the weeks she visited. For this reason it was sometimes difficult to tell how the teacher's awareness and apparent discomfort with the researcher's presence affected her behavior in the classroom, and Solot sometimes felt certain that a specific comment by the teacher was made for her benefit only.

Animal Dissection in Education

From the perspective of a physician involved in clinical practice, education, and research, I have come to the conclusion that killing and dissecting animals is not only unnecessary but also counterproductive in the training of physicians and scientists.

—David O. Wiebers, M.D.

4.1 Introduction

This section deals exclusively with the use of already-dead animals in education. The prevalence of animal dissection in education is discussed first, followed by an examination of humane issues and environmental concerns surrounding the procurement of animals for dissection. Then follows a critique of arguments made in defense of dissection, and finally, an exploration of the availability and effectiveness of alternatives to animal dissection. For humane, sociological, pedagogical and environmental reasons, The HSUS believes that animal dissection should be eliminated from the precollege curriculum and from university education except where absolutely necessary (e.g., veterinary training).

4.2 Prevalence of Dissection

The United States

The most common use of animals in education is for dissection (Mayer and Hinton 1990). Official figures for the numbers of animals dissected in American schools are not available because there is no regulatory requirement to report dead animals either at supply houses or at educational facilities. Based on an estimate that about 75 percent of American high school students participate in animal dissections, Orlans (1993) estimated that close to six million vertebrate animals are dissected in U.S. high schools alone each year and that about three million of these animals are frogs. Orlans's estimate seems accurate; a survey of 1,000 U.S. adults conducted in May 1999 by the National Anti–Vivisection Society found that 78 percent of respondents under the age of fifty-five reported that animal dissection was part of their education (ORC 1999).

The numbers of invertebrate animals used is probably greater (Orlans et al. 1998), especially if one includes the innumerable fruit flies killed in "morgues" (dishes of oil) in genetics courses. When animal use in postsecondary education, specialized training programs, and elementary and middle school is included, the annual educational toll on animals in the United States is probably close to ten million vertebrates and over ten million invertebrates.

In addition to frogs, other commonly dissected species include cats, fetal pigs, rats, minks, pigeons, turtles, snakes, salamanders, bony fish (usually perch), dog-fish sharks, lampreys, crayfish, locusts, earthworms, roundworms, clams, starfish, and barnacles. An HSUS unpublished review of the "preserved specimens" section of a major biological supply company catalog (WARD'S catalog 1995) found 171 different species, 31 vertebrates and 140 invertebrates. In addition to animals available through biology supply companies, a relatively small number of teachers obtain animal parts from supermarkets or slaughterhouses, including chickens' wings, cows' eyes, hearts, and lungs, and sheep's brains.

While reliable statistics are lacking, per capita dissection rates appear to be higher in the United States (and Canada) than anywhere else in the world. It is likely that the volume of animal use in education is proportional to that in research, and the United States easily ranks first in the latter category (Shapiro 1998). Orlans (1993) estimates that three out of four American students will dissect at least one animal by the time they graduate from high school. A BSCS survey in 1982 revealed that 65 percent of biology teachers reported spending at least five hours of the course with preserved specimens, and in many schools students perform dissections of a range of invertebrate and vertebrate specimens in ascending phylogenetic order (Russell 1987). When *The Science Teacher,* a magazine published by the NSTA, surveyed its readers in 1989, only 21 percent of the respondents (number not known) said they never dissected. Of the 79 percent who did dissect, 90 percent reported doing more than one dissection yearly, with some reporting up to fifteen dissections a year.

Dissection in the precollege curriculum is not limited to high school. At Algonquin Middle School, in Illinois, for example, seventh grade students in the life science class are required to dissect five animals: frog, crayfish, starfish, clam, and earthworm; a fetal pig dissection is offered for extra credit (Schmidt 1999). Middle school teachers who attend annual NABT and NSTA conventions frequently report that they or other teachers at their schools are conducting dissections of frogs and invertebrates, and there are reports of the spread of earthworm and insect dissection into elementary schools (Clifton 1992; Duncan 1999). Welch and Luginbill (1985) describe having their middle school students dissect, cook, and eat squid purchased from the supermarket.

There are signs of a growing trend toward having elementary-level children dissect animals. In 1997 The Smithsonian Institution presented a workshop on squids for four- to six-year-olds; among the activities was participation in "dissecting real specimens with scissors." In the summer of 1999, the "College for Kids" program at Tulsa Community College ordered frogs, earthworms, cow eyes, and grasshoppers for four- to eight-year-olds to dissect. A "Blood and Guts" class at Discover Science Summer Camp, in Asheville, North Carolina, offers dissection of frogs, cow eyes, and sheep hearts. The HSUS relies on members and constituents to alert them of these announcements, and it is fairly certain that they represent only a small sample of the actual dissections being done across the country.

In secondary schools, however, there has been in recent years a gradual but steady trend toward teachers dropping dissection from their course requirements (Gilmore 1991b) and students requesting alternatives. According to the NABT, the number of students who dissect each year is declining as educational trends dictate removing dissection from science curricula. Solot (1995) interviewed several science teachers, who noted an increase in students' awareness of animal rights arguments and a corresponding increase in the number of students who base their objections to dissection on these arguments. Kathy Frame, education project coordinator of the NABT, has attributed the decline of dissection to cost and accountability (Solot 1995).

Europe

Internationally there is a dearth of reliable figures on animal use in education, though some European nations keep better records than does the United States on animal use in research. In the United Kingdom, for example, extensive data on animal use are kept, but dissection of a dead animal is not defined a "procedure" by the British Home Office, so there are no official figures for the numbers of animals dissected there (Cochrane and Dockerty 1984). The only estimate of numbers of animals dissected in British schools was reported in a study by the Royal Society/Institute of Biology Working Party (RS/IOB 1975); based on numbers of preserved animals shipped to schools by a biology supply company, they estimated that 100,000 rats, 45,000 dogfish sharks, and 40,000 frogs were used in 1974. These numbers were thought to be higher by the early eighties, at which time more students were studying advanced level biology (Cochrane and Dockerty 1984). While the numbers for Britain provided by the RS/IOB 1975 study and by Cochrane and Dockerty (1984) do not include numbers of freshly killed specimens, they still pale compared with U.S. numbers, even when adjusting for population size.

Nevertheless, enough information exists in Europe to make broad comparisons. Animal dissection is still fairly common, but it doesn't hold the prominent position it enjoys in North American schools. Rates of animal use in elementary through secondary levels of education are considerably lower in Europe (van der Valk et al. 1999), and several countries have passed legislation prohibiting dissection and invasive live-animal exercises at these levels (see section 6.5). In postsecondary education, where animal use is not prohibited, it is estimated that several hundred thousand vertebrate animals are used yearly throughout Europe (ibid.).

International trends in overall laboratory animal use (in research, education, and testing) show significant declines during the past two decades. Shapiro (1998) summarizes these declines for six countries: Netherlands (40 percent decline from 1978 to 1990); Switzerland (eight consecutive years, 1984-1991 inclusive); West Germany (50 percent from 1981 to 1991); Italy (55 percent from 1978 to 1989); United Kingdom (58 percent from 1979 to 1993); and Canada (38 percent from 1977 to 1989). While these declines are probably most attributable to changes in animal testing and research, it is reasonable to assume that educational uses also contribute to these trends.

4.3 Procurement and Animal Suffering

The principal objections to the use of animals for classroom dissection are (1) concern for the way animals are treated before they arrive in the classroom, and (2) concern for the effect the exercise has on students' values and attitudes toward life (see chapter 3). With an annual education demand for close to ten million vertebrate animals and a comparable number of invertebrates in the United States, supplying the bodies of dead animals (usually termed "preserved specimens") is a large and thriving business. In the United States, at least twenty companies supply dead and/or living animals for use in education. Some of these companies (e.g., WARD'S, Nasco, Fisher Scientific) are large and successful, producing hefty, glossy color catalogs selling a broad range of educational materials in addition to preserved/live animals. The largest U.S. company, Carolina Biological Supply Company (CBSC), employs approximately 400 people, has annual sales of more than $25 million, and reportedly doubles in size every six years (Robinson 1996). CBSC was started in 1927 when its founder, Thomas Powell, began selling amoebae and frogs he collected. At the other end of the spectrum are small, family operations, such as Niles Biological and Hazen Farms, which deal strictly in the supply of animal specimens and have only a handful of full-time employees.

Information about the procurement of animals for use in dissection is notoriously hard to obtain in both the United States (King 1994; Solot 1995) and Canada (Zierer 1992). Nevertheless, some investigations have been made, and the remainder of this section summarizes what is known.

Frog Supply

Gibbs et al. (1971) conducted an in-depth study to document the conditions of the capture and warehousing of frogs bound primarily for dissection. The authors were concerned that supplies of frogs were dwindling; frogs caught up in the supply showed "a steady decline in the quality of life"; resulting shipments of frogs were routinely in "extremely poor health"; and scientific uses were compromised as a result.

Gibbs et al. (1971) found that crude handling methods and negligent transport conditions were the primary contributors to these problems. All of the frogs were captured in the wild, and the authors point out "the most basic misconception [that] the laboratory frog is . . . a domestic animal raised on 'frog farms'" (1027).

The animals were taken from populations throughout North America, in a network extending thousands of miles into Canada and Mexico. Most were kept alive between the time of capture and the time of shipping to the classroom or laboratory. At the time of capture, frogs were kept in large sacks or cages. As many as 100 frogs were kept in each sack for up to a week or more, the only care being intermittent spraying with water. Eventually, the frogs were put into large tubs of water where they were kept for periods ranging from days to months depending on the season and the demand for shipments. During this period, the frogs were provided no food. Frogs shipped during the summer likely had gone without food for a week or more between capture and arrival at a school; in the early spring, frogs may not have eaten for more than six months. Live frogs were usually shipped 50 to a box lined with sphagnum moss. In the summer months, most frogs were "hot," meaning that they were overheated and hyperactive often to the point of convulsion.

Gibbs et al. (1971) describe the high mortality rates that resulted from these conditions. Many of the frogs not initially crushed or "broken" during the rigors of capture, transport, and shipping in the sacks, died of starvation or disease in the unnatural and unsanitary holding tanks. On average, 15 percent of frogs were either dead or obviously injured following their initial transportation from collection site to the sorting depot. Gibbs et al. (1966) found that it was not uncommon for more than two-thirds of frogs being kept alive in the school or laboratory to be dead within the first week of their arrival. This article was not the result of antagonism towards the frog trade. One of the authors (Emmons) was an employee of a supply company dealing in frogs, and the authors expressed concern that experimental use of live frogs was declining at that time.

There is little to indicate that conditions of frog capture, transport, and storage have changed substantially since Gibbs and his colleagues published their study in 1971. Field investigations conducted between 1997 and 1999 by The HSUS suggest that the only significant change is that a much larger proportion of frogs is now killed before shipment to schools.

Rana Laboratories, a CBSC supplier located in Brownsville, Texas, is representative of The HSUS's findings. A November 1997 interview with the plant manager revealed that Rana purchases well over 100,000 pounds of leopard frogs yearly and an unknown quantity of bullfrogs. The animals are taken from wild populations, primarily near the west coast of Mexico, and kept without food during the holding period prior to distribution. Live frogs are stored in trays inside coolers maintained at 50 degrees Fahrenheit and are shipped in boxes. Mortality rates during shipment can be high, particularly when held up at the U.S.–Mexico border during harsh weather conditions.

The frogs are killed at unpredictable intervals by dropping them into a solution of alcohol and water. The animals take fifteen to twenty minutes to die. An interview with the owner of another supply company, Cyr's Biology, located in Ponchatoula, Louisiana, yielded similar information, with the additional note that live frogs are sometimes stored in the coolers for three months. In its report on euthanasia, the American Veterinary Medical Association makes no mention of immersion in alcohol as a means of killing amphibians (AVMA 1993).

PETA's Investigation of CBSC

With the launch of the modern animal rights movement a decade after Gibbs et al.'s article, the response of biological supply companies towards outside inquiries about the sources of animals sold for dissection became increasingly guarded. Consequently, the most detailed information regarding industry practices in recent years has been gleaned by animal protection organizations conducting undercover investigations. Their findings have tended to reinforce concerns that neglect and abuse pervade the procurement of animals for dissection.

In 1989 two employees of the organization People for the Ethical Treatment of Animals (PETA) worked for several months at CBSC headquarters in Burlington, North Carolina, following complaints of animal abuse at this facility. One of the investigators, Bill Dollinger, was able to secure employment in the section of the company that handles animals after they arrive at the facility. Using a hidden camera, he videotaped several disturbing scenes of live cats arriving at the facility in crowded wire cages.

The quality of Mr. Dollinger's video is adequate to make some reliable assessments of conditions at CBSC. The behavior of the cats as they are poked with a long metal hook from one cage to another and then into the gas chambers (which used 100 percent carbon monoxide in bottled form), suggests high levels of stress in these animals. The handling is rough and noisy, and the cats' movements are jumpy and skittish. Many of them have crouched postures and nervous, wide-eyed facial expressions. In his written log, Mr. Dollinger (PETA n.d.) describes the following related observations:

- up to twenty cats per cage (measuring approximately 4' x 1.5' x 1') in vehicles lacking ventilation
- a cat giving birth while being gassed
- a cat meowing after being gassed
- the movements of unborn kittens visible in the bellies of pregnant cats following gassing

These are violations of basic humane standards. Bottled carbon monoxide (CO) is accepted by the AVMA (1993) for euthanasia of cats, but The HSUS (1994), deems it "absolutely unacceptable" for use on cats who are old, young (under four months), sick, or injured. Gas chambers must never be overcrowded, and they should be designed to minimize stress and to allow for the appropriate separation of animals (ibid.). The random sourcing of cats killed at CBSC and the stressful, crowded conditions of gassing indicate that these caveats are not met.

Cats are not the only species observed being subjected to pain and/or distress at CBSC. Another videotaped scene shows a rat wriggling while being strapped into a restraining device and catheterized. During the initial stages of formaldehyde infusion, the vigorous, coordinated movements of the rat strongly suggest that the animal is at least partially conscious. Other excerpts from Mr. Dollinger's written (PETA n.d.) and videotaped evidence includes:

- a live dog trying to crawl from beneath a pile of dead dogs in the back of a truck
- a rabbit, still breathing, being catheterized and embalmed
- shipments of live pigeons left on a loading dock for six and one-half hours in small cardboard boxes

- embalming of living frogs
- a large tray of apparently fully alive adult crabs being injected
  with a liquid thought to be formaldehyde preservative

The behavior of some of the CBSC employees is sometimes callous and sadistic, as evidenced by the following descriptions by the investigator (PETA n.d.):

- an employee spits on a rat after strapping the wriggling animal to
  a restraining device
- an employee laughs as a cat convulses after being
  hooked up to an embalming board
- a cat is bludgeoned to death by an employee after the cat bit him
- an employee deliberately prolongs the drowning of a rabbit by repeatedly
  pulling the animal from the water as he is about to drown
- employees play catch with a rat before drowning him

In a follow-up investigation by ABC News of CBSC practices aired in October 1990, Al Wise, one of CBSC's major suppliers of cats at that time, is filmed while turning the bulldozer he is driving towards a reporter and charging him before ramming an ABC News van as it flees the scene. Two years after the ABC News report, the United States Department of Agriculture (USDA) charged Mr. Wise with obtaining cats illegally and falsifying his records. The charges were resolved on July 7, 1993, when Mr. Wise agreed to an order banning him from operating as an animal dealer for ten years (AWA Docket No. 93-118).

The question of whether or not some cats were still alive at the time of embalming following gassing was one of approximately ten charges of violations under the Animal Welfare Act (AWA) brought by the USDA against CBSC in 1991. During the hearing two USDA veterinarians testified that several cats were still alive, but two veterinarians retained by CBSC testified that all the cats were dead when embalmed. The USDA judge ruled in favor of CBSC on the basis of their experience with and knowledge of embalming animals. Movement of the cats on the embalming boards was attributed to muscular movements that occur during infusion with formalin and to the pressure (10-12 pounds per square inch) at which the embalming fluid entered the cats' circulatory systems.

In the end, CBSC was held accountable for its failure to maintain complete records of the acquired animals, for failures in sanitation and maintenance of enclosures, for inadequate storage of animal food, and for failure to keep its premises clean and free of accumulations of trash. The company was assessed a civil penalty of $2,500.

Other Investigations

A 1989 study by Bonner et al. (1989) examined the supply of red-eared slider turtles for classroom experiments. Thirteen turtles ordered from Connecticut Valley Biological Supply Company (Southampton, Massachusetts), where they were observed being warehoused in crowded conditions, exhibited a range of maladies not found in a control group of eight wild-caught turtles. These included hemorrhaging from the shell; paralysis; swollen, inflamed eyes with purulent drainage; respiratory problems; diarrhea; marked weight loss; and overall lethargy and apathy. Three of the warehoused turtles died from illness during the ten-day acclimation period of this study.

In 1994 the World Society for the Protection of Animals (WSPA) sent two investigators to Mexico following a report of a vehicle carrying two thousand preserved cat specimens in Mexicali. It was discovered that cats were being rounded up from the streets and killed by putting ten cats into a sack and drowning them or by affixing the sack opening to a car exhaust pipe. The bodies were embalmed and then shipped to the United States for school dissection (WSPA 1994). The man in charge of collecting the cats admitted that a large proportion of them were probably owned (WSPA 1994; WSPA n.d.). The company, Preparation of Animal Material for Scholarly Study (PARMEESA), was filling a shipment quota of 1,500 cats per month and had been in operation for approximately 20 years, supplying dead cats (as many as 3,000 per week) and other species to several American biological supply companies, including Fisher EMD, Delta, Frey Scientific, and Sargent Welch (WSPA n.d.).

In 1995 authorities raided a chicken farm near Monterrey, Mexico, and found 800 dead cats. Workers at this facility told health officials that the cats were killed by "sticking a piece of wood in their mouths to keep them still and cutting their throats"(Associated Press 1995). Television crews on the scene filmed 20 dehydrated live cats panting in what was described as a sweltering shack. The cats were being shipped to the United States for use in school dissections. The owner of the facility was not charged with animal cruelty but for possessing too many dead animals and for mishandling chemicals. In a previous raid of the same ranch earlier that year, 500 dead cats had been found, and similar operations were reported in other Mexican border states (ibid.).

It is not certain to what extent these findings are representative of procurement practices in the biological supply trade. The specific investigations cited above were spawned by complaints lodged by employees or witnesses, which could mean they were atypical cases where things had gone awry. On the other hand, many factors suggest that inhumane practices are commonplace and perhaps routine in the supply industry, including the lack of regulatory oversight, closed-door policies of the suppliers, and the potential for lack of humane care when living animals will be sold dead (Orlans et al. 1998). To date, the supply companies have not publicly broached the procurement issue other than to defend themselves when under attack (CBSC 1994).

Animal Shelters

While wild populations are numerically the largest source of dissected animals, there are several other sources of animals used in dissections. Some animal control facilities choose to sell euthanized cat and dog carcasses to biological supply houses for use in dissections. At one time pound seizure laws in more than a dozen states required shelters to relinquish un-adopted animals to research labs and schools when requested to do so. In the past few decades, however, most of these laws have been repealed, making it either illegal to transfer animals from shelters for laboratory use, or discretionary on the part of the shelter.[1]

In light of the euthanasia of several million unwanted cats and dogs in U.S. shelters annually, it could reasonably be argued that these carcasses be put to educational use in our schools. This is no simple matter, however. The HSUS condones transfer of euthanized animals from shelters to research or educational institutions under only very limited circumstances. First, no transactions of live animals should occur, and any animal involved must have been euthanized due to either mortal illness or injury, or because no suitable home could be found for the animal within a reasonable time. Second, animal cadavers may be transferred only when the animal's former owner has been informed of this policy and has given consent. Full public awareness of any animal transfer policy is vital to maintaining public trust in animal shelters. Regardless of owner consent, however, shelters not wishing to supply animal carcasses to institutions should not be compelled to do so.

Third, such transfers should not involve elementary, middle, or high schools. The HSUS opposes the practice of animal dissection in precollege classrooms for numerous reasons. At the college and graduate levels, the need for animal cadavers is obvious in veterinary training, for instance, but the cadavers should come only from euthanized animals and no animal should be raised or killed specifically for use in dissection. Fourth, transfer of animals from animal shelters should not involve the exchange of money. The existence of so-called "surplus" cats is a product of pet overpopulation, a problem needing resolution more than exploitation. Millions of cats are killed yearly in U.S. shelters because there are not enough homes for them all. When there is money to be made in dealing in their carcasses, there may be less incentive to address overpopulation. There is also the perception that the shelter would rather gain from this tragedy than invest their monetary resources toward resolving it.

Farmed Animals

Animals raised and killed in the meat industry are another source of dissection materials. Parts of animals, such as sheep brains and cow eyes, are sometimes used. Fetal pigs, removed from pregnant sows following slaughter, have become one of the most commonly used animals for school dissections. Viewed as by-products of the meat industry, these late-term fetuses have been called "the perfect specimen"(Nebraska Scientific n.d.). Nebraska Scientific alone processes more than 300,000 fetal pigs per year (ibid.), and annual school use of fetal pigs is estimated at half a million, though there are signs that declining availability may force this number down (Lewis 1999). Many teachers also use chicken wings and other animal parts that can be bought at local grocery stores (personal communications at science teacher conventions).

Certainly, the notion of using animals (or parts of animals) who are already dead and whose alternate destination may be an incinerator or rendering plant may seem sensible. As Nebraska Scientific (n.d.) points out in its brochure promoting the fetal pig as a dissection specimen: "The fetal pig was never born; it did not 'die' for dissection purposes. For those concerned about the use of live animals in scientific study, these fetal pigs are a viable alternative."

However, there are serious humane concerns with this source of animals. The conditions in which a majority of animals raised for human consumption live on factory farms today have been widely criticized as inhumane (Mason and Singer 1990; Rifkin 1992). Conditions of transport from farm to slaughterhouse are routinely bad, causing significant numbers of animals to die in transit. Of 200,000 pigs deemed unfit for human consumption in the United States in 1994, 74,000 died during transport (Marbury 1994). And in the abattoir itself, an in-depth investigation by Eisnitz (1998) documented routine abuse and some instances of sadistic cruelty.

When a school purchases fetal pigs from a biological supply company, or a teacher buys some chicken wings from the supermarket, the meat and slaughter industries profit from it. Should schools be helping to perpetuate the problems in the raising of animals for meat? Many of the students who conscientiously object to dissection do so on humane grounds. Many are vegetarians. Participation in the dissection of animals that come from the meat industry is not an acceptable option for them.

Fur-Bearing Animals

Classroom dissection of animals from fur farms, while less common, is no less problematic from a humane standpoint. Skinned mink, fox, and rabbit carcasses are available from biological supply company catalogs and the source is identified alongside them. The methods of trapping and killing wild animals for their pelts and methods of raising fur-bearing animals in captivity are inhumane (McKenna 1998). When schools buy these carcasses from supply companies, they provide income for the fur industry. Even if one feels that using these animals is morally acceptable, many students would not do so if they were fully aware of the conditions under which the animals were raised and killed. Many teachers are not aware of the relevant facts, so these issues are not usually discussed in the classroom.

Not only may animals destined for dissection suffer prior to death, their death in itself is harmful (Gilmore 1991a). Killing sentient beings involves a moral cost that needs to be addressed (Regan 1983; Cavalieri and Singer 1993).

4.4 Ecological Concerns

In this era of heightened environmental awareness, it is hard to find anyone who would openly disparage environmental protection and stewardship. Animal dissection runs counter to the aims of environmental protection by exploiting already vulnerable wild animal populations and by using hazardous chemicals.

Frogs

The frogs used for dissection in North American schools are almost always taken from the wild. At the time of their 1971 article on the supply of leopard frogs (*Rana pipiens*) and bullfrogs (*Rana catesbeiana*) for education and research, Gibbs et al. (1971) reported that U.S. suppliers were shipping approximately 9 million frogs (326.5 metric tons) annually for educational and research purposes alone. All of these frogs were being taken from the wild. The authors reported that frog populations had declined an estimated 50 percent in the prior decade, and concluded that "though frog-catching is probably not the major cause of the drop in the frog population, its influence certainly cannot be considered negligible."(1028)

Declines in frog populations have apparently worsened since then, making these animals something of a cause celebre of global environmental concern (Phillips 1994; Blaustein and Wake 1995). While some frog populations continue to thrive, many are declining and some have recently gone extinct. Numerous factors are thought to be contributing to the demise of certain frog populations, including habitat destruction, ultraviolet rays breaking through a dwindling ozone layer, fungal disease, air and water pollution, and human consumption (Blaustein and Wake 1995).

Theoretical arguments that frog populations can sustain themselves in the face of heavy human predation have proven false (Phillips 1994). Because frogs play such key roles in their ecosystems both as predators and prey, the detrimental effects of their overexploitation extend through the ecosystem. The taking of frogs from the wild for the frog leg trade was banned in India in 1987 in part because their declines were considered to be contributing to surging insect populations (Jayaraman 1987).

Along with dusky leopard frogs *(Rana berlandieri)*, leopard frogs and bullfrogs are the most commonly used species in American schools, and both are in decline. According to Emmons (1980), Nasco's collection of leopard frogs exceeded 30 tons in an average year prior to 1972 but dropped to only five tons in 1972 due to declining availability. Well-documented declines of these two species have been reported in both U.S. and Canadian populations (Hine et al. 1981; Vogt 1981; Kingsmill 1990; Klassan 1991), and Souder (1998) reports that the leopard frog may have disappeared completely from British Columbia. Collection for educational uses has been cited as contributing to bullfrog declines in both Canada (Kingsmill 1990) and the United States (Vogt 1981). Vogt (1981) points to the long time needed by bullfrogs to attain sexual maturity as hastening their declines and recommends a ban on all commercial collecting of the species.

Orlans (1993) estimated that 3 million frogs are dissected in U.S. high school classrooms each year. Additional frogs are used in postsecondary as well as middle school dissections. Efforts to turn the tide for frogs should involve both curbing human exploitation of wild populations and fostering appreciation and respect for their kind. Classroom frog dissection undermines the pursuit of these goals.

Sharks

The spiny dogfish shark *(Squalus acanthias)* is a small shark species (an individual weighing over five pounds is considered large) with populations off both the Atlantic and Pacific coasts of the United States. Exploitation for human consumption has gone up markedly in recent years, with average yearly landings of about 6,200 metric tons from 1977 to 1989, rising to 19,300 and 22,600 metric tons (about 20 million individuals) in 1992 and 1993, respectively (Rago 1994). *S. acanthias* is particularly vulnerable to exploitation because of its slow reproduction. The age at which females attain sexual maturity is higher than that of humans, and may be as old as twenty years (about eleven years for males). Gestation is also prolonged (two years), with litters ranging from two to fifteen pups.

Given the long period it takes for this species to mature, there would be an expected lag of a decade or more before population declines would be reflected in catch rates. Yet, the Ocean Wildlife Campaign, a consortium of environmental groups including the Natural Resources Defense Council, World Wildlife Fund, the National Coalition for Marine Conservation, and others, believes there is already sufficient fisheries data to demonstrate that the Atlantic population of *S. acanthias* is being threatened by overfishing (Wilmot et al. 1996). The National Marine Fisheries Service considers this species "fully exploited" (Rivlin 1996). Because the species is notably vulnerable, the Ocean Wildlife Campaign recommended in 1996 that the U.S. Fish and Wildlife Service list *S. acanthias* as threatened under the U.S. Endangered Species Act.

Notwithstanding its ecological plight, *S. acanthias* has been and remains a popular species for school dissections. Biological supply companies pay fishermen for the dogfish sharks the companies market to schools for dissection (Robinson 1996). At least seven major U.S. biological supply companies sell *S. acanthias*. Bob Iveson (personal communication, 25 October, 1999), a scientist with WARD'S Biological, estimates the total number of these fish sold for dissection each year to be 100,000. Notwithstanding other arguments against animal dissection in schools, the tenuous ecological status of *S. acanthias* alone ought to discourage biology teachers from ordering this species in future.

4.5 Formaldehyde Exposure

Classroom dissection of preserved animals almost invariably involves a degree of exposure to formaldehyde. Used to embalm and preserve the dissected specimens, formaldehyde presents both immediate and potential long-term threats to the health of those participating in dissections. Formaldehyde (or formalin) is classified as a "toxic and hazardous substance" by the United States Occupational Safety and Health Administration (OSHA).

Formaldehyde is irritating to the upper respiratory tract and eyes. Concentrations of 25 to 30 parts per million (ppm) cause severe respiratory tract injury, and a concentration of 100 ppm is immediately dangerous to life and health. Deaths from accidental exposure to high concentrations of formaldehyde have been reported (OSHA n.d.). High concentrations can also cause permanent vision impairment if splashed on the eye, and prolonged exposure may result in respiratory impairment. Both OSHA and the American Conference of Government Industrial Hygienist standards place the human safety limit of formaldehyde at 1 part per million (ppm) (Young 1984). One part per million (ppm) is also the odor threshold for most people, so if one is using formaldehyde and can smell it, then its concentration exceeds the acceptable level prescribed by these standards (Young 1984).

No student who has ever dissected animals forgets the pungent odor of formaldehyde that accompanies the exercise. OSHA officials have acknowledged that use of formaldehyde as a tissue preservative for school dissections presents a health hazard and warrants the wearing of protective clothing, including gloves and goggles. A May 16, 1990, letter from then Assistant Secretary of Labor Gerard F. Scannell to the Association of American Medical Colleges states, in part: "In addition to the inhalation hazard, solutions of formaldehyde (such as the formalin used as a tissue preservative) can damage skin and eye tissue immediately upon contact. For this reason the standard requires effective protective equipment to prevent skin and eye contact, as well as eye-washes and showers if there is the possibility of splashes to eyes and body"(OSHA Web site *www.osha.gov/*).

Despite OSHA's concern about formaldehyde's hazards, students who dissect animals at schools are provided with little or no protection, and enforcement of OSHA standards is rare. One exception was Mt. Saint Mary College, New York, which was recently fined

$20,000 for various violations of OSHA standards, including exposing employees to formaldehyde and infectious substances (Blumenstyk 1996).

4.6 Defenders of Dissection

In response to growing criticism of dissection and vivisection in education, several articles have appeared explicitly defending these practices.

Schrock (1990)

The main thrust of Schrock's argument for dissection, and the basis for his disdain for alternatives, is that only the former provides the learner with "real material" and "real experience" (Schrock 1990). Schrock points out, correctly, that no model is complete, and that no simulation can replicate an actual organ or organism. Also, he adds, media such as pictures, models, and computer simulations fail to provide the full sensory experience—sound, taste, smell, and touch—that dissection provides (ibid.). For Schrock, dissection is "the only way to provide meaning to communications about anatomy, physiology, and health" (ibid., 15).

Schrock laments "the abysmal level of anatomical/medical understanding among American citizenry," and calls for a doubling of time spent in anatomy labs to correct it. But there is no evidence that such understanding parallels the amount of time spent dissecting animals. In Sweden and Norway, for example, where dissection is almost nonexistent in the high school biology curriculum, students have attained significantly higher scores in scientific literacy tests (Gibbs and Fox 1999) than in America, where dissection is widespread. There is also no evidence that dissection is the only way to gain such understanding. To the contrary, studies of dissection alternatives find them to be at least as effective for imparting anatomical/medical knowledge (section 4.7).

The importance Schrock places on "real" experiences can also be rebutted. The "realness" of most preserved animal specimens is reduced by a number of factors related to death, embalming, and shipping in tightly packed containers. Simulations provide some level of realness (Schrock acknowledges this). Most importantly, Schrock provides no compelling case that realness is the measure of a learning tool's effectiveness. Throughout science education, and education in other disciplines, we learn by using representations, symbols, and abstractions. Students learn about genes in genetics labs, atomic structures in organic chemistry, Cladism in systematics, and—to use one of Schrock's examples—hydrostat cells without ever seeing any of them in concrete form.

This is not to scoff at real experience. It is, of course, invaluable, and indispensable in many cases (e.g., surgical training—see section 5.4). But ultimately, Schrock's appeal to realness is moot, for the principal objection to animal dissection is the harm inflicted on the animal during procurement (section 4.3), and not that the animal is real. Indeed, The HSUS and other animal protection organizations encourage the judicious and humane use of living animals in education. In a study by Bauhardt (1990) and reviewed by Killermann (1998), a group of 125 sixth grade students who studied living invertebrates by handling them and not harming them showed significantly greater improvement in knowledge, attitude, and interest levels than did a group of 118 students who used preserved specimens and supplementary materials. Where real experience with animal tissues and organs is necessary, then ethical sources of animals can and should be found (see "ethical dissection," section 4.7).

Perhaps most revealing in Schrock's argument against alternatives to dissection is his reference to "Lysenkoism," which he believes is analogous to philosophical objections to harming animals for education. Trofim Lysenko was a Russian scientist who rose to prominence during the Stalin era because his notions of inheritance appealed more to communist ideals than did Darwinian evolutionary principles. As a result, Russian scientists who championed reality-based Western genetics were banned from research, and Lysenko's dogma cost Russia thirty years of progress in genetic research (Medvedev 1971). Schrock believes that replacement of animal dissections with computer simulations and other alternatives represents a similar abandonment of real science "to make our 'science' match with popular or expedient social and political views" (Schrock 1990, 13).

The underlying assumption of Schrock's Lysenkoism theory is that alternatives to dissection are being adopted in response to pressures from the animal protection sector. He provides no evidence for this tenuous notion, nor does he acknowledge the cost savings and the strong educational performance achieved by many simulations, which seem more likely causes for their adoption than ideological pressure.

Pancoast (1991)

In an article published in *Teacher Magazine,* Pancoast (1991) offers several defenses for the use of animal dissection in the classroom. She alludes to the billions of animals killed for meat in the United States (approximately eight billion per year) and notes that the use of animals for research and education constitutes only about 0.3 percent (24 million) of animal consumption. Without stating it outright, Pancoast tries to convince readers that they need not be concerned about some twenty-four million animals because eight billion is such a greater number. If this logic were sound, then we would not try to prevent airline crashes because car accident rates are far higher. It is also tantamount to claiming that a 6'1" professional basketball player is short, because most other professional players are taller. Pancoast is not the only writer to use this argument (e.g., Hamm and Blum 1992).

Pancoast also tries to justify animal dissection by pointing out that fifty-four of seventy-six Nobel Prizes (71 percent) in medicine and physiology in this century were based on animal research. Even if animal use has played a vital role in breakthrough research, it is a considerable leap of faith to claim that its completion hinged on whether or not students dissected animals in high school class. Pancoast's Nobel figure is contestable; Stephens's (1987) analysis of Nobel Prizes determined that alternative methods played a key role in the research of fifty of the seventy-six (66 percent) laureates. Clearly there is subjectivity in estimating the role of animal experimentation in prize-winning research.

Pancoast is even more adamant that students not choosing careers in the life sciences should get exposure to animal dissection. Without any supporting data, she views the exercise as unforgettable, and that it may be these students' only chance to appreciate the complexity and intricacy of living creatures. There are two assumptions here: (1) that dissection is the only way to appreciate the complexity of the living organism and (2) that dissection invariably provides such an appreciation. Both assumptions are false.

Dissection is only one way that a willing student might be able to appreciate the complexity and intricacy of living animals. There are many others. The complexity that Pancoast refers to can only be the *gross structural* complexity of body systems, organs, and some tissues. One is not able to observe or appreciate either behavioral complexity or fine structural complexity from a dead, preserved animal. By comparison, computer simulations allow students to view many levels of complexity unavailable to the dissector. The CD-ROMs on the human body produced by ADAM (Animated Dissection of Anatomy for Medicine) software, for example, show not only gross structural anatomy in high detail, but also contain histology images, animations, and video clips of body processes unobservable during gross dissection of a living or dead organism. (For a more detailed discussion of dissection alternatives, see section 4.7).

Although some students may dissect a dozen different animal species during their biology schooling, they may not be struck by the complexity of the anatomy they observe. The bodies of preserved animals are often misshapen as a result of packing, the internal organs—through which living fluids have long since stopped flowing—tend toward a monochromatic gray cast, and the depth of study is almost invariably superficial, with attention given only to gross anatomy of the dissected specimen.

Nevertheless, Pancoast may be right that dissection is unforgettable, but perhaps not for the reasons she hopes. When Shapiro (1992) asked Maine legislators what they recalled of their encounters with high school dissection, they tended to have vivid recollections only of the more visceral aspects of the exercise: the pungent smells and the ambivalence they felt about slicing into the bodies of once-living animals with scalpels and scissors. Solot (1995) made a similar observation from her qualitative study of dissection at a Rhode Island high school, noting that striking visual images of the exercise seemed to be more indelible than the anatomical relationships that formed the academic basis for the lesson.

Holden (1990)

Holden (1990), writing for the journal *Science,* likens efforts to make dissection optional for students to the efforts of religious fundamentalists to stifle the teaching of evolution. This is a weak analogy. Dissection opponents are unhappy with a particular *method* of teaching biology and are not interested in doing away with the study of life-science itself; creationists oppose the very *subject* of evolution regardless of how taught. While there is nothing unscientific about learning with computer technology, 3-D models, or videotape (or indeed, by studying animals noninvasively), the same cannot be said of the scientifically untestable notion of a divine creator (Mayr 1982). A substantial and growing body of published scientific literature shows that so-called alternatives are competitive with dissection for teaching life science; the same does not apply to replacing evolution with creationism, because it is not a parallel pursuit. Finally, while objections to evolution are based on such nebulous concepts as faith and soul—neither of which is accessible to scientific inquiry—objections to dissection rest on the very real issues of animal pain and suffering, and human and nonhuman violence (see chapter 3).

Hamm and Blum (1992)

Hamm and Blum (1992), of Stanford University Medical School's Department of Comparative Medicine, make the common error of exempting dissection from regulatory concern because of the mistaken belief that it does not involve animal pain or distress (see also Marquardt 1993). As already discussed, animal dissection involves a great deal of animal pain and distress; it occurs usually before the animals reach the facility where they are dissected. The authors also point out that there are worse fates for animals consumed for other uses than for those harmed for education, where they are "generally handled with far greater solicitude and care." Evidence from the biological supply trade suggests otherwise, but in any event, ethical conduct requires that we strive to avoid causing animal pain and distress, regardless of degree. Hamm and Blum (1992) do recommend that discussion of ethical and moral considerations for using animals in education be carefully integrated into every student's course of study.

Biological Variation

The value of animal dissection as a way of demonstrating biological variation is frequently noted in support of dissection and as a way to devalue computer simulations, which tend to show only a single idealized specimen (Berman 1984; Morrison 1992). Biological variation could, of course, be illustrated using video, photographic, and/or computer-based learning materials. However, even in the absence of such resources, the students in a biology class present a ready source of interindividual biological variation, and there are numerous noninvasive ways to study and appreciate this variation (e.g., Orlans 1977; Russell 1978). Plants are another readily available source of subject material to study intraspecies variation (e.g., Dalby 1970; Keown 1994). Finally, it is not clear that dissection classes do, in fact, commonly use the specimens to demonstrate variation.

Other Arguments

Some writers have resorted to trivial arguments to try to justify harming animals for an education exercise. In an article titled "The Importance of Animal Dissection," Lord (1990) asks: "Why does not the dissection of a flower or seed arouse the same sympathies in dissection opponents as the dissection of a frog or rabbit?"

In implying that animal dissection is the moral equivalent of plant dissection, Lord disregards the moral import of an organism's having a nervous system and being able to experience pain and distress.

Howard (1993) goes so far as to claim that those who breed animals to kill them are promoting the interests of the animals: "None of these [dissected] animals would be born if not wanted, and they have a quality life and die humanely rather than live nature's torturous life. From the standpoint of a quality life, the need for this resource produces an improvement of life for some individuals of these species."

Howard is fond of the Victorian notion that nature is "red in tooth and claw," that "carnage pervades the natural world" (McInerney 1993), and that suffering is the wild creature's lot. He has used it to defend a diversity of human exploitations of animals (Howard 1990; Balcombe 1994). It is the same flawed logic of Pancoast (1991) and Hamm and Blum (1992) that one type of harm done to animals is acceptable because there are worse and greater harms that befall them.

It appears as though there is a common misconception among dissection proponents such as Howard (1993) and Hamm and Blum (1992) that most animals used for classroom dissections are raised in the laboratory. When Lord (1990) discusses the "four major ways" that supply houses procure dissection specimens, the capture of individuals from wild populations—the most common method of procurement and probably the most troublesome from a humane standpoint—is not even among them.

4.7 Alternatives to Dissection

The educational aim of dissection is primarily to impart knowledge on the anatomy and physiology of either the species of animal being dissected or animals (including humans) in general. Berman (1984) lists a number of other aims of animal dissection exercises, including understanding relationships between animals of different species, grasping the concept of individual variation, understanding the relationship of structure to function, gaining insight into the relationship between an organism and its environment, and teaching respect for life. Wheeler (1993) argues that dissection is a worthwhile skill in itself, and that the difficulty in performing dissections well helps to teach students that there are practical difficulties and limitations in the pursuit of scientific knowledge. Wheeler adds that dissection exposes students to a method that has played an important historical role in the acquisition of biological knowledge, and that it provides a concrete, nonabstract personal experience.

Dissecting animals has potential for imparting all of the above educational benefits to certain students, even teaching respect for life (see "ethical dissection," below). However, if we are going to continue to include anatomy as a mainstay of basic biology education, a key "value" question is not whether or not dissection can achieve these aims, but rather whether there are other methods—methods that do not carry the moral burden of destroying animal life—that can satisfy them as well or better. If there are, then moral concern should dictate that animal dissection be replaced in schools.

There has been, in the past twenty years, a spectacular proliferation of new learning materials that can be used in place of animal dissection. These dissection alternatives are dominated by computer-based programs. A sampling of popular programs currently being used in the United States includes:

- ScienceWorks: *DissectionWorks* (earthworm, crayfish, fish, frog, pig, cat)
- Pierian Spring Software: *BioLab* series (pig, frog, invertebrate [earthworm, crayfish, sea star], fly [genetics])
- Tangent Scientific: *DryLab* series (frog, crayfish, perch, rat, fetal pig, earthworm)
- Digital Frog International: *Digital Frog, Digital Frog 2*
- NeoTek: *CatLab*
- Animated Dissection of Anatomy for Medicine: (ADAM) several programs,

including a series of five physiology modules

Whereas all computer programs up to the early 1990s were stored on diskettes (or occasionally on videodiscs), practically all (including all of those listed above) are now available as CD-ROMs. Some of these programs simulate the actual step-by-step performance of a dissection, with the user making "cuts" along the specimen with the mouse-controlled cursor. Many of these programs also provide a variety of other information to supplement and enhance the lesson. Animated sections may comprise actual film or artists' renderings of functioning systems at the organ, tissue, cellular, or molecular level. At least one program (*3-D Body Adventure,* by Knowledge Adventure) displays "fly-throughs" of the skeletal and circulatory systems of the human, in which the viewer tours these systems in three-dimensional space as if piloting a miniature airplane. On-line self-evaluation modules—some of which are randomly generated—are also available on many of these programs, allowing the user to evaluate his/her knowledge level and chart his/her learning progress.

Three-dimensional models, usually made of hard or soft plastic, provide tactile, textural, and spatial experiences not currently available with computer programs. Frogs are the most commonly modeled species, but fetal pigs, cats, sharks, rats, starfish, chickens, perch, and locusts are among the others. The human body is represented by an enormous range of sophisticated and life-size models. Denoyer-Geppert, a Chicago-based company, is notable for its range of hand-painted plastic models of the human. A recently developed process called "plastination," in which a deceased animal's tissues are chemically replaced by plastic, allows preservation of minute detail in gross anatomical features and produces a durable model for repeated use. Ohio State University is one of several universities that have begun to plastinate animal carcasses and to use them in their courses (Richard Tallman, personal communication, 1998).

Videotapes and charts provide moving and stationary images of animal dissections. The *Cat Anatomy Instructional Videotape Series,* contained on eight separate videotapes and distributed by Micron BioSystems, features an exhaustive, several-hour-long survey of cat anatomy. Other species available on videotape include the frog, fetal pig, crayfish, earthworm, perch, starfish, clam, and grasshopper. By using freshly killed animals, the *Vertebrate Dissection Guides* video series (rat, pigeon, frog, shark), produced in the United Kingdom, and the BioCam charts (pig, rat, frog, earthworm, crayfish, clam, perch, starfish, grasshopper, and pig heart/sheep brain) provide especially detailed and true-to-life images.

Not surprisingly, the advent of alternatives in education has been accompanied by studies to assess their effectiveness as learning tools. The general approach of these studies has been to compare them to traditional, animal-based methods, and to date, there are close to thirty such studies published in the scientific literature. Table 4.1 provides an annotated list of these studies.

Table 4.1
Published Studies Comparing the Performance of Alternatives with Traditional Animal-Based Learning Methods in Life Science Education[a]

Authors	Study Subjects	Principal Findings
Cohen and Block 1991	10 U. S. undergraduates (psychology)	Students who studied feral pigeons in a city park scored equally well on evaluations as did students who studied operant conditioning with rats in a traditional lab.[b]
Dewhurst and Meehan 1993	65 U.K. undergraduates	Students using computer simulations performed equally well as students using traditional approaches in physiology and pharmacology laboratories.[b]
Dewhurst et al. 1994	14 second-year U.K. undergraduates	Six students working independently with a computer program gained equal knowledge, at one-fifth the cost, to eight supervised students using freshly killed rats.[b]
Downie and Meadows 1995	2,913 first-year U.K. biology undergraduates	Cumulative examination results of 308 students who studied model rats were the same as those of 2,605 students who performed rat dissections.[b]
Guy and Frisby 1992	473 U.S. prenursing and premed students	Performance of students using interactive videodiscs was not significantly different from that of students in traditional cadaver-demonstration labs.[b]
Jones et al. 1978	100 freshman U.S. medical students	Learning performances of students using films, computer-assisted instruction, and prosected human cadavers were the same as those of students taught by traditional lecture and dissection.[b]
Kinzie et al. 1993	61 U.S. high school students	Findings suggest that an interactive videodisc was at least as effective as dissection in promoting student learning of frog anatomy and dissection procedures.[b]
Leathard and Dewhurst 1995	105 U.K. preclinical medical students	No significant difference was found in the performances of students who used a traditional live-animal laboratory and those who used a computer simulation on intestinal motility.[b]
Leonard 1992	142 introductory U.S. biology undergraduates	In the use of videodisc or traditional laboratories, no significant difference was found for students' laboratory grades. However, the videodisc group required one-half the time.[b]
Lieb 1985	23 U.S. high school students	Posttest scores were equivalent for students who dissected earthworms and those who received a classroom lecture on earthworm anatomy.[b]
Prentice et al. 1977	16 U.S. physician's assistant students	Based on student learning performances, the authors concluded that use of labeled sequential slides of anatomical dissections provided a viable alternative to dissection.[b]
Strauss and Kinzie 1994	20 U.S. high school students	Two groups of high school students performed equally on a test following either animal dissection or interactive videodisc simulation.[b]

Table 4.1 (continued)

Authors	Study Subjects	Principal Findings
Dewhurst and Jenkinson 1995	20 U.K. undergraduate teaching institutions	Use of computer packages saved teaching staff time, were less expensive, were an effective and enjoyable mode of student learning, and significantly reduced animal use.[c]
Fowler and Brosius 1968	456 U.S. high school students	Students who watched films of animal dissections (earthworm, crayfish, frog, perch) demonstrated greater factual knowledge of these animals than did students who performed dissections on them.[c]
Henman and Leach 1983	U.K. undergraduate pharmacology students	Students using biovideograph performed significantly better on post-laboratory tests than those participating in the organ-based laboratories.[c]
Huang and Aloi 1991	150 introductory U.S. biology undergraduates	Students using a computer-assisted interactive videodisc system that included dissection simulations performed significantly better than students who had not used the computer-aided instruction.[c]
Lilienfield and Broering 1994	252 U.S. medical and graduate students	Students who used computer simulation achieved a significantly higher grade in the cardiovascular section of the final exam than their classmates.[c]
McCollum 1987	350 U.S. high school biology students	Approximately 175 students taught frog structure, function, and adaptation via lecture performed better on a posttest than did approximately 175 students taught by doing a frog dissection.[c]
More and Ralph 1992	184 U.S. biology undergraduates	Biology knowledge of about 92 students using computer courseware increased more than did that of approximately 92 students using traditional animal-based laboratories.[c]
Phelps et al. 1992	Undergraduate U.S. nursing students	Students who studied using an interactive video program on cardiac output principles performed better on a posttest than did students taught by lecture and live-animal physiology laboratory.[c]
Samsel et al. 1994	110 U.S. medical students	Students used both computer demonstrations and animal (dog) demonstrations, and rated the former higher for learning cardiovascular physiology.[c]
Matthews 1998a	20 U.S. biology undergraduates	Eight students who dissected fetal pigs scored significantly higher on an oral test with prosected fetal pigs than did twelve students who studied on a computerized pig (*MacPig*).[d]

[a] Excluding veterinary schools (see table 5.2).
[b] equivalent performance
[c] statistical significance favoring alternatives
[d] statistical significance favoring traditional method

Studies comparing animal labs and nonanimal alternatives have found that both high school students (Lieb 1985; McCollum 1987; Kinzie et al. 1993; Strauss and Kinzie 1994) and college students (Leonard 1992; More and Ralph 1992; Phelps et al. 1992; Dewhurst and Meehan 1993; Dewhurst et al. 1994; Downie and Meadows 1995) learn just as well using alternatives as they do using traditional animal-consumptive methods. Similar results have been found for training in veterinary medicine (Fawver et al. 1990; Johnson et al. 1990; White et al. 1992; Holmberg et al. 1993; Greenfield et al. 1995), medicine (Jones et al 1978; Lilienfield and Boering 1994; Samsel et al. 1994; Leathard and Dewhurst 1995), prenursing and premedicine (Guy and Frisby 1992), pharmacology (Henman and Leach 1983), and physician assistant (Prentice et al. 1977). Several of the above studies showed statistical significance favoring alternatives (see table 4.1), while only one favored the animal laboratory.

Several additional studies, while not evaluating student learning performance directly, have nonetheless reported student preferences and time and cost savings for alternatives to traditional animal labs. In their study of 82 U.S. veterinary students, Erickson and Clegg (1993) found that students rated computer-based active learning the highest of fourteen learning methods for basic cardiac teaching and electrocardiograph interpretation. Use of computer packages by 20 British teaching institutions saved teaching staff time and money, were an effective and enjoyable mode of student learning, and significantly reduced animal use (Dewhurst and Jenkinson 1995). In a study involving 110 U.S. medical students who used both computer demonstrations and animal (dog) demonstrations, the students rated the former higher than the latter for learning cardiovascular physiology (Samsel et al. 1994).

A study by Pavletic et al. (1994) compared surgical abilities of 12 graduates from the Tufts University veterinary class of 1990 who had participated in an alternative small-animal medical and surgical procedures course with 36 of their counterparts. The subjects were rated for surgical competency by their employers at the time of their hiring and again twelve months later. No significant differences were found on either occasion for any of the measures, which included ability to perform common surgical, medical, and diagnostic procedures; attitudes toward performing orthopedic or soft tissue surgery; confidence in performing procedures; or ability to perform procedures without assistance.

These studies are far from flawless, and they do not cover the extensive range of alternatives applications now available for educational use. But collectively they provide a strong case that alternative learning methods are as effective pedagogically as are traditional methods that use animals, and they suggest that alternatives are in a number of ways better than animal-based exercises (Balcombe 1997b; Pope 1997).

The only study published to date that found a significantly higher performance from students (college undergraduates) using animal dissections over those using an alternative was reported by Matthews (1998a) (see table 4.1). However, the dissection alternative used in this study (the computer program *MacPig*) is too rudimentary for college-level biology classes (Balcombe 1998), despite apparent manufacturer's claims to the contrary (Matthews 1998b). As such, it is not surprising that students using the computer program, who had not had any experience with preserved fetal pigs, scored worse (41 percent compared with 82 percent) on the oral exam—which used a prosected fetal pig—than did students who dissected fetal pigs (ibid.). The computer-using students scored higher than the dissecting students on the computer quiz (75 percent compared with 66 percent), though the difference was not statistically significant.

Computer-Assisted Learning

Today most alternatives to dissection are computer-based, and computer-assisted learning (CAL) is assuming an increasingly dominant role in education in general. One of the seven priorities of the U.S. Department of Education is that "every classroom will be connected to the Internet by the year 2000 and all students will be technologically literate" (U.S. Department of Education 1997).

Twenty years ago Kulik et al. (1980) conducted a meta-analysis of 54 published studies of CAL versus traditional teaching in postsecondary classrooms and found that students using CAL performed significantly better (by 3 percent) on examination scores. By 1996 Kulik had analyzed 250 such studies and reported that gains from CAL were generally enough to move an average student in the 50th percentile to the 64th percentile while simultaneously working at a 34 percent faster pace (Beyers 1996) A meta-analysis of 28 studies by Bosco (1986) of Interactive Videodiscs (a technology being rapidly replaced by CD-ROMs) rated their efficacy for learning as favorable overall. The Educational Testing Service recently released a report showing that learning improves when technology is used effectively to engage higher order thinking skills (Wenglinsky 1998).

The reported benefits of CAL in the life sciences include active involvement of students, even in large classes; less time needed to present information and for students to master it (Teyler and Voneida 1992; Dewhurst and Jenkinson 1995); greater cost-effectiveness (e.g., Dewhurst and Jenkinson 1995; Leathard and Dewhurst 1995); and self-paced learning that puts students in control of the learning resource (Nosek et al. 1993; Leathard and Dewhurst 1995; Erickson and Clegg 1993). Faculty members in veterinary medicine and in education at Kansas State University found that CAL increased opportunities for active learning, was less demanding of teacher resources, decreased live-animal use, and improved learner skills in problem solving and information handling. In a survey of eighty-two veterinary students, the subjects rated active learning experiences highest, with the computer labs receiving the highest scores. It should be noted that computer programs need not necessarily rely on static, synthetic data. Not only can random variation be built into the program (Nab 1989), but some programs (e.g., Pankiewicz 1995; Intelitool 1998) also use data from the students' bodies.

Cost of Alternatives

Teachers and school administrators often cite the cost of alternatives as a reason for their not being implemented (Balcombe 1997a). In fact, animal dissection is often more expensive. A cost analysis by The HSUS found that for a typical school's needs, the cost of providing animal specimens for dissection was often greater than the cost of purchasing a range of reusable alternative materials (table 4.2). Depending on numbers needed, the initial cost of computer programs, videotapes, and three-dimensional models may or may not be higher than a shipment of preserved animal specimens, but the alternatives can be used repeatedly, while the specimens must be replaced after a single use. Providing a single class with bullfrogs for dissection can cost a couple of hundred dollars (Griffith 1991). Recent shortages in the supply of fetal pigs to schools have raised prices to the point that a single fetal pig CD-ROM (featuring on-screen dissection, video clips, and built-in quizzes) may cost less (as low as $18.30 each) than a single fetal pig specimen (up to $23.74) (Lewis 1999). A comparison of costs for an instructor-based versus a computer-based physiology lab found that the live lab cost more than twice the amount (£860 and £320, respectively), without considering the cumulative savings from being able to re-use the computer-based modules in succeeding years (Leathard and Dewhurst 1995).

Table 4.2
Costs: Dissection Exercises versus Alternatives to Dissection for Commonly Dissected Animals

Cat

Alternatives	Cost	Dissection	Cost
Anatomy model (x 2)	$800	High-cost animal ($48.45 x 135)	$6,541
Dissection video (39 minutes)	$70	Low-cost animal ($23.75 x 135)	$3,206
CatWorks (x4)	$360	64-page dissection manual (x30)	$285
CatLab (CD-ROM) (x 4)	$200	Supplies	$1,500
64-page dissection manual (x 30)	$285		
VCR	$150		
TOTAL COST	**$1,865**	**HIGH COST**	**$8,326**
		LOW COST	**$4,991**

Alternatives can possibly save between $3,126 and $6,461

Bullfrog

Alternatives	Cost	Dissection	Cost
Frog Inside Out video (67 minutes)	$159	High-cost animal ($11.25 x 135)	$1,519
Pictorial atlas (x 30)	$269	Low-cost animal ($5.97 x 135)	$806
Great American Bullfrog (x 2)	$1,310	Pictorial atlas (x30)	$269
The Digital Frog (CD-ROM) (x 4)	$600	Supplies	$1,500
DissectionWorks (CD-ROM) (x 4)	$240		
BioCam dissection chart (x 30)	$90		
VCR	$150		
TOTAL COST	**$2,818**	**HIGH COST**	**$3,288**
		LOW COST	**$2,575**

Alternatives can possibly save $470 and possibly cost $243

Table 4.2 (continued)

Fetal Pig

Alternatives	Cost	Dissection	Cost
Fetal pig model (x 2)	$590	High-cost animal ($14.85 x 135)	$2,005
BioCam dissection chart (x 8)	$90	Low-cost animal ($3.15 x 135)	$425
DissectionWorks (CD-ROM)(x 8)	$1,600	56-page dissection manual (x 30)	$285
Fetal pig anatomy (26 minutes)	$70	Supplies	$1,500
56-page dissection manual (x 30)	$285		
VCR	$150		
TOTAL COST	$2,785	HIGH COST	$3,790
		LOW COST	$2,210

Alternatives can possibly save $1,005 and possibly cost $575

Note: These figures are based on a hypothetical school's needs for a three-year period. Reusable materials (dissection tools, trays, computer programs, models, charts, etc.) are treated as a one-time purchase. Costs are based on a ratio of two students per animal dissected (45 animals a year, 135 animals over three years). This comparison assumes that the school already has computers and CD-ROM players, but no VCRs. Because dissection manuals are needed for dissection but are also useful stand-alone study guides, they are included under both Alternatives and Dissection headings. Low and high prices of preserved animals were obtained from the Nasco Science 1999 Catalog and the alternatives (1999 prices) were selected from available lists, catalogs, and databases. Numbers of alternative materials were derived based on the assumption that students would not be using all alternatives at one time.

Availability of Alternatives

Alternatives to animal dissection, and relevant information about them, are readily available. They are conspicuously present in the exhibit halls of science teacher conventions, and most manufacturers have Web sites describing their products in some detail. Furthermore, resourceful teachers can gain access to dissection alternatives at little or no cost. There are at least four animal protection organizations in the United States that loan alternatives to dissection for temporary use with no cost to the borrower except return postage. The HSUS Humane Education Loan Program has more than 100 different CD-ROMs, videotapes, 3-D models, and charts for loan. The National Anti–Vivisection Society (NAVS), the American Anti–Vivisection Society (AAVS), and the Ethical Science and Education Coalition (ESEC) each have similar loan programs. Internationally, the European Network of Individuals and Campaigns for Humane Education (EuroNICHE) operates an alternatives loan program, as does the Australian office of Humane Society International. Both The HSUS and AAVS have recently launched programs that actually donate CD-ROMs to schools with a demonstrable commitment to using them. The manufacturers of many of these materials have "product preview" policies, allowing the prospective buyer to order and try them out for a few weeks, with the option of returning them to the company at no cost.

There are several databases accessible through the Internet that provide descriptions, prices, and ordering information for thousands of alternative learning materials. Two excellent databases that focus specifically on alternatives in education are:

- NORINA (Norwegian Inventory of Audio-Visuals):
  [http://oslovet.veths.no/NORINA/search.html]
- AVAR (Association of Veterinarians for Animal Rights): *[http://AVAR.org]*

Collectively, these two databases contain information on close to five thousand alternatives, and they allow searching by scientific discipline, learning level, type of material being sought (e.g., videotape, computer simulation, 3-D model), and others. There are also two printed compendia of alternatives to animal use in education, EuroNICHE's *From Guinea Pig to Computer Mouse: Alternative Methods for a Humane Education* (Zinko et al. 1997), and ESEC's *Beyond Dissection: Innovative Tools for Biology Education* (Larson 1998).

In the face of available, cost-effective alternatives that measure up well against animal dissection, the persistence of dissection in the school curriculum is a curious phenomenon. A possible reason could be the cultural transmission of traditional learning methods, wherein a teacher simply uses the approaches with which he/she was taught. Another is that there is currently a lack of resources and materials to teach teachers to be comfortable with new computer-based technologies (Sampson 1998).

Ethical Dissection

Animal dissection could be acceptable if the specimen is procured ethically. It is the deliberate harm inflicted on so many animals to make dissection available to students and the usual lack of any ethical context for the exercise that warrant criticism. Creative, concerned teachers can give their students experience with dissection and/or close contact with living anatomy without compromising a desire to do no harm to animals.

Ordering preserved animal specimens from biological supply houses will not usually suffice. When teachers ask representatives of biological supply companies about the source of the animals sold for dissection, they are apt to get blanket reassurances that the animals are handled legally and humanely. Teachers should not accept this, as the evidence from closer scrutiny of these operations indicates that there are significant costs in environmental harm and animal suffering (see section 4.3). Teachers should demand specific source information, with supporting evidence. By doing this, suppliers are made aware that teachers care about the humane and ethical aspects of procurement, and it may encourage supply companies to improve their record-keeping and record-sharing practices.

But even if the company can provide evidence that its animals are procured in legal and humane ways, that may not mean that the source is ethical. Instead of purchasing animals of unknown origin from biological supply companies, using animals who have died of natural causes is a preferred option (Morton 1987), provided sanitary sources can be found. An example is depicted on a video on alternatives in education by EuroNICHE (*Alternatives in Education* 1999), which documents Norwegian veterinary student Siri Martinson driving to a nearby farm to collect a sheep who died of natural causes, then returning to the lab to conduct a detailed anatomical study of the animal. In the United States, one teacher video-taped her veterinarian's necropsy of a horse who had died unexpectedly and now uses this resource with students (Mayer and Hinton 1990). The use of companion animals who had died of natural causes resolved a dispute that arose at the University of Pennsylvania school of veterinary medicine in the mid-eighties when two students refused on moral grounds to participate in labs that harmed healthy animals (Shapiro 1987).

More could be done to secure deceased companion animals as an ethical source of dissection specimens. Approximately ten to fifteen million companion animals are euthanized at shelters and veterinary hospitals every year (Patronek and Rowan 1995). While the cadavers of some of these animals are cremated or buried at the owners' request, the majority are turned over to renderers or disposed of in large-scale cremation. Similarly, at least tens of thousands of injured wild animals die at veterinary clinics and wildlife rehabilitation centers each year. These animals might be made available, with appropriate disease control safeguards, to schools. In all cases, students would be informed of the origins of the animals so that they understand that the animal was procured in a caring, ethical manner.

Taking one's students to observe surgeries at a local veterinary clinic is another option (Balcombe 1997b).[2] While this arrangement places limits on the number of observers at any given time and would not normally allow students to make physical contact with the animal, it has the advantage over dissection that the animal is living, that the anatomy is fresh and in full color, not preserved, and that the procedure is being done in the interests of the animal. It is also increasingly possible to take one's students to a hospital to observe live operations in progress from an overhead observation gallery, which may also feature video monitors. Similar galleries are used at some veterinary schools, such as the University of Florida, where students observe equine surgeries (Gretchen Yost, personal communication, August 1999).

Finally, human cadavers offer yet another ethical source of a dissection specimen. Human cadavers are made available through consent of the individual in life. While typically expensive, human cadavers play an important role in nursing and medical education, and they have been used effectively in a variety of undergraduate disciplines (Peterson 1993) as well as in high schools (Wharton 1996).

Outdoor Study of Animals

As an alternative to dissection, outdoor study provides limitless opportunities for on-the-spot, hands-on learning (Heintzelman 1983; Russell 1987; Hancock 1991; Harding 1992), and living organisms—particularly invertebrates—can be studied noninvasively both in and out of the classroom (Hairston 1990; Ogilvie and Stinson 1992; Schwartz 1992a, b). The belief that observing animals in the wild helps teach reverence for life is also widely held by humane educators (Russell 1996). Animal studies conducted in natural settings have a number of advantages over study in the classroom. First, and perhaps foremost, the organisms being studied are observed in their full evolutionary context; not only are natural phenomena not suppressed as they may be in captivity, but unnatural behaviors that may result from captivity and confinement are avoided. Thus, students get the opportunity to observe animals in the ecological setting to which they are adapted.

Another advantage is that students can learn firsthand that studying animals in the outdoors presents challenges to the scientist. They learn to appreciate that the animals are not ready and willing to cooperate in the studies they have designed and that the quest for information requires creativity and flexibility when it becomes apparent that the animals have not read one's study proposal! Many educators will likely view this sort of challenge as a disadvantage, given the limited time they have to provide an education to their students, but the instructive power of such experiences can be great (see chapter 2). There are a number of good resources for relatively simple outdoor studies that overcome this obstacle (e.g., Heintzelman 1983; Hancock 1991; Harding 1992; Ogilvie and Stinson 1992).

In contrast to outside observation, keeping animals in-class has the advantage of providing students with ready access and direct contact with the living organism. There are many useful observational studies that can be conducted noninvasively in the school, such as simple genetics, behavior, maturation, learning, and food preference (Office of Technology Assessment 1986; Morton 1987). There are, of course, caveats to keeping animals in classrooms: these include welfare concerns for animals inadequately housed and cared for (Morton 1987), the potential for disease transmission or injury to students, and the potential to undermine the development of students' respect for the special relationship between an animal and its environment. For these reasons, The HSUS (1993) recommends that only domestically bred animals with limited space and housing requirements be kept in classrooms and that keeping wild animals in the classroom is generally inappropriate. In rare cases, native wild vertebrates whose habitats can be easily simulated (e.g., toads, turtles) may be acceptable for short-term captivity in the classroom (ibid.)

4.8 Recommendations

For humane, sociological, pedagogical, and environmental reasons, The HSUS believes that animal dissection should be eliminated from the precollege curriculum and from university education except where absolutely necessary (e.g., veterinary training). However, realizing the pervasiveness of this activity, a realistic set of steps towards this goal follows:

1. Animal dissection should be eliminated from the precollege curriculum.

2. All procurement of animals for dissection should be from ethical sources, such as animal shelters, veterinary clinics, and wildlife rehabilitation facilities. Guardian consent programs should be established so that cats (and other companion animals) who have died or been euthanized for medical or humane reasons can be donated from shelters or veterinary clinics to schools for educational use. These cadavers should replace the supply of cats from random sources, fetal pigs from slaughterhouses, frogs from wetlands, etc.

3. The USDA, which is responsible for inspecting biological supply companies (classified by the USDA as "Class B Dealers"), should begin requiring biological supply companies to provide annual reports. These reports should include the numbers and species of animals killed or arriving dead at the facility, numbers sold to schools for educational use, and methods of capture, transport, handling, and killing of the animals.

4. Biological supply companies should be required to conduct environmental impact assessments prior to collecting from wild animal populations.

5. Students should be informed of the specifics regarding the sources of animals used in the classroom, including methods of capture, transport, handling, and killing of the animals.

6. Dissection of species whose populations are known to be over-exploited and/or in decline (e.g., leopard frogs, bullfrogs, spiny dogfish sharks) should be discontinued.

7. Students involved in dissections should be provided with gloves, masks, and safety instruction to minimize the hazards of exposure to formaldehyde.

8. Science teacher training should, without exception, include training in the use of computer simulations and other alternatives resources, including alternatives databases and loan programs.

---

[1] Only two states (Minnesota and Utah) and a few smaller jurisdictions (e.g., the city of Houston, Texas) currently (1999) mandate pound seizure.

[2] The author remembers vividly the size, color, texture, and the highly vascularized outer lining of the distended bladder of a domestic cat whose surgery to relieve a blocked urinary tract he observed in 1979. Equally memorable was the remarkable volume of fluid this organ held.

Live-Animal Use in Education

I think the biggest limitation for [veterinary] students is getting past the idea that something is an "alternative.". . . We need to make them normal and typical, not "alternative."

—Lara Marie Rasmussen, D.V.M.

5.1 Introduction

This section examines the use of living animals in education and available alternatives to such use. Specifically, the focus is on uses that will harm the animals involved. It is the position of The HSUS that living animals can and should play a vital role in education, but that their use—with few exceptions—should be limited to situations that are noninvasive and nonharmful. An important exception is for the training of veterinarians, but even here, invasive procedures can be learned in a manner that takes the animals' interests into consideration.

5.2 The Life Sciences

Precollege Education

Invasive uses of live animals still occurs regularly in American schools, though it is less common than animal dissection in precollege education, and is prohibited in some states (e.g., California, Florida, Illinois, Maine, Massachusetts,

New Hampshire, New York, and Pennsylvania) (Leavitt and Beary 1990). Internationally, several countries have enacted laws that prohibit live-animal experimentation by students (e.g., Germany, Iceland, the Netherlands, Poland, South Africa, and the United Kingdom). A few other countries' laws suggest implicitly that invasive live-animal use is rare or nonexistent (e.g., Argentina, Slovak Republic, and Sweden).

Just as record-keeping practices in America make it difficult to estimate accurately the amount of animal use for dissection in American schools, it is also not possible to know with any precision the frequency of invasive live-animal use. No survey has ever been done on this subject. What is known must be gleaned from curriculum outlines and materials, student complaints, journal articles, and newspaper reports.

One form of live-animal experimentation in the classroom that has occurred quite commonly in precollege classrooms is nutrition studies. As of 1987 one biology supply company advertised nine different nutritional deficiency diets available for in-class rat studies (Russell 1987). For at least two decades now, the Dairy and Nutrition Council (1987) (self-touted as "the nutrition education people") has marketed a science kit for fourth through eighth grade school children with the intention of demonstrating the nutritional value of cow's milk. Titled "The Great Grow Along," the method involves providing two rats with different diets over a period of a few weeks. The effect of the diets is measured by regularly weighing and sizing the rats.

The Great Grow Along is not a good science teaching tool. First, real scientists would never use a sample size of one or two animals because it is impossible to accommodate biological variability or use statistics with so few experimental subjects. Second, the underlying premise of the study—that cow's milk is an important part of a healthy human diet—is questionable and subject to growing dispute (Karjalainen et al. 1992; Iacono et al. 1998). Despite the claims of the dairy industry, cow's milk is no more natural for a human child (or a rat) than is human milk for a calf. Third, the assumption—implicit in this project—that bigger is better (in this case, in body size) is an unhealthy one to be impressing upon schoolchildren, especially in a nation beset with the highest obesity rates in the world. Fourth, the assumption that what goes for a rat goes for a human is equally tenuous; the nutritional needs of rats and humans are far from equal.

It is not known how commonly The Great Grow Along is being used in schools today. The HSUS had two complaints about it from parents in Missouri and Wisconsin in 1998. That it is used at all indicates the seductiveness of "canned" projects in a school science curriculum.

Another exercise involving live animals that is still commonly carried out in elementary classrooms is chick hatching. While less obviously harmful to animals than nutritional deprivation studies, chick hatching projects present a number of humane problems in spite of the best intentions of the teachers who conduct them. Successful incubation of chicken eggs requires meticulous care; mother hens rotate their eggs up to thirty times a day and help to maintain proper temperature, humidity, and ventilation conditions for healthy embryo development. Replicating this level of care in the classroom is difficult. The result is that some chicks die before they hatch or emerge from their eggs in a deformed or sickly state. This is disturbing to children.

Inevitably, the chicks who survive grow to be too big to keep in the classroom. It then becomes very difficult to find appropriate places for them to go. If sent home with students, they are often unwelcome and may be treated inhumanely. Sometimes the animals are drowned or suffocated. Most often, the birds end up at animal shelters where they are usually euthanized. These problems are outlined in a NAHEE (National Association for Humane and Environmental Education) booklet of alternative activities, titled *For the Birds!: Activities to Replace Chick Hatching in the K-6 Classroom* (DeRosa 1998).

Some teachers have begun to post on the Internet classroom exercises that involve invasive uses of live animals. Access Excellence Program, *www.gene.com/ae/MTC>*, a place for science teachers to share their ideas, is one such place where these postings may be found, though it should be noted that these sorts of postings tend to be ephemeral, and none of the following examples could be found six months after they were originally discovered in the fall of 1998. A Delaware-based high school teacher included a study exposing fish to tobacco among a series of projects she conducts with her science class. Though she was careful to note that the fish do not succumb to their exposure, it is apparent that the exercise is not in the fish's best interests. Similarly, a Wisconsin-based high school teacher has her students study the effects of temperature variation on respiration rates in goldfish. Two other examples involve dissection of living insects. One describes an exercise in which flour beetles *(Tenebrio molitor)* are "inactivated" by spending ten minutes in a freezer before being wax mounted, submerged in Yaeger's saline, then dissected by students. Another describes the dissection of a live cricket (St. Remain 1991). In light of uncertainty regarding pain perception in insects, the previous exercises may not be problematic in humane terms, but the same may not be true of the effects on children's sensibilities when they are instructed to harm and kill living creatures (see chapter 3).

Postsecondary Education

At the college level, invasive and/or harmful uses of live animals are relatively more common, most notably in the fields of physiology, psychology, pharmacology, and zoology. Two traditional physiology labs that remain fairly common in American colleges are the frog gastrocnemius muscle and the turtle heart preparations.

In the frog muscle physiology lab, live frogs (usually leopard frogs, *Rana pipiens*) are rendered brain-dead by pithing. Frog pithing is still occasionally done by inserting one blade of a pair of scissors into and across the mouth of a (live and fully conscious) frog and slicing the top of the head off. Sometimes the animal is "double-pithed" by destroying the spinal cord as well with a thrust of the probe through the vertebrae. Following pithing, the gastrocnemius muscle of the frog is dissected out of the body and hooked up to an electrical recording device so that various aspects of muscle response to electrical stimulation can be observed and recorded. A Web site that shows the steps involved in isolating a frog nerve can be found at *<umech.mit.edu/freeman/6.021J/schindjr/lab/frog-lab-home.html>*.

In the turtle heart lab, a turtle (usually a freshwater species, such as the red-eared turtle, *Chrysemys scripta elegans*) is pithed, then the plastron (undershell) is removed with a circular saw so that the living heart can be observed. Various chemical compounds are applied directly to the heart to observe stimulating and retarding effects on the heartbeat; the vagus nerve in the animal's neck may also be manipulated to observe the effects on heart function.

It is difficult to know the prevalence of pithing exercises in American schools today. It is safe to say that the practice is quite rare in high schools and is more usually done in undergraduate physiology courses. Robinson (1996) reports that Carolina Biological Supply Company ships out between 75,000 and 90,000 live frogs per year. Some of these animals probably go to scientific research projects and some to pithing labs. While the pithing procedure itself is usually done out of view of the students, this is not always the case. Many students who witness pithing have strong aversive reactions to it (see section 3.4). The HSUS is aware of at least two recent student campaigns (at the University of Georgia and Cornell University) to end pithing labs.

In addition to pithing labs, many other invasive uses of live animals occur in advanced undergraduate courses. According to 1996 figures (the most recent available) released by the Canadian Council on Animal Care (CCAC 1999), 300 animal experiments reported under the heading of "Education and Training of Individuals in Postsecondary Institutions and Facilities" were classified as in the category E of severest pain. Data of this sort are not available in the United States, but comparable animal use practices occur, especially in advanced life science courses.

Such a course is taught in Ohio State University's (OSU) microbiology department. The HSUS obtained information on this course in 1995 from the Institutional Animal Care and Use Committee (IACUC) minutes sent to The HSUS by an Ohio-based animal rights group (Protect Our Earth's Treasures), which had recently won a lawsuit granting them access to OSU's IACUC minutes.

The course, titled "Principles of Infection and Host Resistance," accommodates up to 125 students per year. The instructor's 1995 request for IACUC approval described five invasive animal labs, involving 475 mice and 20 rabbits:[1]

- 20 rabbits given Freund's complete adjuvant and bled via intracardiac puncture
- 20 mice killed by cervical dislocation (neck breaking), then dissected to obtain bacterial slides and swabs from abdominal organs
- the lethal bacterium *(Streptococcus pneumoniae)* injected into the stomach cavities of half of a group of 135 mice (the remainder were injected with a saline solution as a control); mice observed every forty-eight hours for ill effects
- 250 mice each receive four injections into the stomach cavity over a four-week period; all are exposed to the infectious bacterium *Salmonella typhimurium;* all mice are killed in this lab
- 65 mice are injected twice with the infectious bacterium *Staphylococcus aureus*

The occurrence of invasive live-animal procedures bears more relation to the preferences of the instructor than to the learning requirements of the discipline itself. In all of the life science disciplines, one finds many examples of programs where animals are not used. The most salient example is the use of animals in medical training, where about half of the 126 U.S. medical schools do not use animals (section 5.4).

5.3 Alternatives to Live-Animal Use

Most live-animal experiments in education can be replaced by nonanimal alternatives (Nab 1989). Because these experiments have been conducted repeatedly, year after year, the parameters and results are known, and the experiments can thus be simulated by other learning methods. This approach does not compromise the scientific rigor of the lesson, because it is the learning process that counts, not the experimental results themselves (ibid.).

Nab (1989) lists advantages of computer simulations over invasive live-animal labs:

- students must be active or else nothing happens
- students can study many factors at one time and vary parameters on a large or small scale
- the simulated "animal" can be repaired; students can make "fatal" mistakes without losing the experiment
- the computer can give feedback, provide hints, and offer help
- slow processes can be accelerated and fast ones slowed down
- experiments can be repeated at any time and almost any place
- the simulation can be simplified to negate confusing side effects, which can hinder the understanding of basic principles
- fewer animals are used

These advantages are borne out by the results of published studies that find student learning performance when using computer-based (and other) alternatives to be at least equal to that of students using live animals (see table 4.1).

In addition to the advantages of computer simulations, Nab (1989) also mentions a few limitations. These include:

- a mathematical model is never complete and cannot exactly simulate the complexity of a living biological system
- simulations do not provide student contact with living animals
- computer simulations cannot train manual skills, like surgery and handling

As Nab observes, the first limitation above is not important for most educational uses, which usually involve the study of basic principles that most computer simulations are designed to mimic. That simulations deprive students of contact with animals is not a criticism of simulations; an instructor who values student contact with real animals will ensure that students get it whether or not he/she makes use of computers.

Physiology is traditionally one of the heaviest users of invasive procedures in animals. A survey by the Association of Chairmen of Departments of Physiology (Greenwald 1985) reported that most physiology faculty believed that no alternative could fully replace live-animal use in education. Respondents also reported that alternatives limited students' exposure to working with live subjects as well as student experience with interaction in the complex systems of a living thing.

These points are self-evident, and they do not say anything about the efficacy of alternatives. One could as soon criticize live-animal use on grounds that it takes away time that could be spent using the alternatives, which have features unavailable to the student who studies only animal subjects (see above).

At the instructional level, the use of animals is based more on personal preference than on pedagogical necessity, as there are many examples of animals being replaced altogether in physiology curricula. Kerstin Lindahl-Kiessling of Sweden's Uppsala University, for example, designed the physiology course for biological science students without any animal experiments. She believes that animals are not needed for good physiology teaching because there are so many other ways to demonstrate physiological principles (Alternatives in Education 1999). Sewell et al. (1995) provide an example of the effective use of a multimedia computer package to replace the frog heart and sciatic nerve–gastrocnemius muscle preparations.

Many other instructors have praised computer-based physiology labs, noting such benefits as teaching students to manipulate ideas like scientists do (Tauck 1992), allowing students to conduct real experiments (Stringfield 1994), motivating students (ibid.; Kuhn 1990), and teaching respect for life (Tauck 1992). Clarke (1987) described the advantages of using simulations over traditional nerve isolation experiments, noting that by avoiding the tedious, often unsuccessful isolation and preparation of the nerve tissue, the simulation allowed much more time to be devoted to the experiment itself, so that students could explore the subject in greater depth. Other studies demonstrating time savings when using alternatives to traditional animal physiology labs include Fawver et al. (1990), Dewhurst et al. (1994), and Brown et al. (1998).

Other notable resources that have successfully replaced traditional live-animal physiology exercises include:

> The Virtual Physiology Series (five CD-ROMs), produced at the University of Marburg, Germany, covers the entire field of nerve-muscle physiology and simulates all of the classic experiments conducted by medical, dental, veterinary, biology, and chemistry students; these programs are in use in both Europe and North America, and faculty response has been enthusiastic (Thieme Interactive n.d.).

> The SimBioSys Physiology Labs use animations, simulations, exercises, and quizzes, and cover general, cardiovascular, respiratory, and renal physiology; over 1,000 physiological parameters can be reproduced; by altering parameters, students gain understanding of how the body works (Critical Concepts, Inc. 1999).

> DynaPulse Systems allows students to monitor their own cardiovascular profiles; also includes a "patient management" system that allows long-term tracking and statistical analyses of students' cardiovascular status (Pankiewicz 1995).

> Intelitool's software series allows students to study respiratory physiology (Spriocomp), muscle contraction (Physiogrip, Flexicomp), and cardiac physiology (Cardiocomp); students generate their own original data from their own bodies, making them both the investigators and the experimental subjects (Intelitool 1998).

Pharmacology is another high user of live animals in education. Loiacono (1998) describes the use of alternatives to replace traditional pharmacology labs at the University of Melbourne (Australia). Traditionally, various drugs were screened for their behavioral effects on animals and the students were expected to produce a profile of these effects for various families of drugs. The alternative, a CD-ROM package titled *Behavioural Pharmacology*, allows the student to review a larger range of drug families, including those such as convulsants and central stimulants that the instructors regarded as ethically untenable for an undergraduate practical class. Other advantages include short video-sequence reviews of the types and uses of behavioral tests, a series of self-assessment tests, additional text-based material, and a presentation format that combines figures of drug structures alongside behavioral effects and allows the student to quickly link to any other part of the program. The instructors report being able to broaden the scope of the class and to incorporate elements that would be too time-consuming in the traditional laboratory setting. This alternative also represents a reduction in animal use. Concomitant disadvantages are that students see only "ideal" responses that do not depict the interindividual variability in drug response, and the students are less involved in the decision-making that accompanies live-animal experimentation. Loiacono (1998) reports that these factors are being overcome with approaches that are more interactive, allowing the student to participate actively in the presented experiment.

At the University of Queensland, Lluka, and Oelrichs (1999) describe 89 percent reduction in animal use between 1980 and 1999 in physiology and pharmacology programs. Among their teaching strategies are recorded experiments, broadcast experiments, simulated experiments, interactive tutorials, and human experiments (with student volunteers). The authors emphasize the importance of knowledgeable instructors, good design of accompanying notes, and the need to "ensure that the students relate to the exercise as a practical experiment and not as a computer exercise"(6).

For the acquisition of practical skills, there are many noncomputer, nonanimal alternatives available (see the following section). When Nab (1989) wrote his article, computer simulations were not yet available to mimic the manual and tactile experience of surgical exercises. However, today, the technology of virtual reality (VR), while not yet widely available, can provide a realistic training experience for many of the practical skills that medical professionals use (Coppa and Nachbar 1997). The VR project at the New York University School of Medicine is now used extensively by faculty and students and plays a vital role in the school's medical curriculum (ibid.).

Ultimately, practical laboratories seek to expose students to the process of doing science and to the types of difficulties and uncertainties that might be encountered. Hands-on experience is also important and any study of biology should definitely include exposure to living animals (including students!). The HSUS argues that a true "respect–for–life" ethic requires that harmful animal use in schools should be eliminated.

5.4 The Health Sciences
Medical School

In the past, the use of live animals has been routine practice in the American medical training curriculum (Foreman 1992). However, recent trends indicate that animal use is declining. According to the Physicians Committee for Responsible Medicine (PCRM), which for the past decade has been pressuring medical schools to replace animal labs with nonanimal alternatives, about half of all 126 U.S. medical schools—including such prestigious institutions as Mayo, Harvard, Columbia, and Yale—now have no live-animal laboratories (PCRM 1998). One clear conclusion that can be drawn from this information is that live-animal use is not indispensable for medical training.

The most common live-animal lab conducted in U.S. medical schools is the "dog lab," in which students perform a series of terminal procedures on anesthetized dogs. Besides dogs, other animals commonly used by medical schools are pigs, cats, and rabbits. Most often, the animal labs occur in the disciplines of physiology, pharmacology, and surgery (Wolfe et al. 1996).

Animals are also used in more advanced medical training. Examples include use of dogs and pigs for Advanced Training and Life Support, use of cats and kittens for intubation training, and use of pigs and dogs for laparoscopy and surgical stapling. Ohio State University's medical school, for example, has been using 120 adult dogs and 120 adult pigs yearly for laparoscopy and surgical stapling of the intestine and stomach (OSU IACUC minutes, March 1995), and as of 1999 (Richard Tallman, personal communication) continued to do so. That any medical institution trains its students without the use of live animals clearly indicates that live-animal labs are not an indispensable part of medical training (OTA 1986).

Alternatives for Medical School

A survey by Barnard et al. (1988) found that live-animal labs existed in the regular curricula of 49 of 93 responding physiology departments (53 percent), 27 of 110 responding pharmacology departments (25 percent), and 15 of 81 responding surgery departments (19 percent). A 1994 survey by Ammons (1995), to which 125 of the total 126 U.S. medical schools responded, showed further declines in live-animal use for all three subdisciplines, to 39 percent, 10 percent, and 17 percent, respectively. Results from a survey by Wolfe et al. (1996), also conducted in 1994, yielded higher percentages for each subdiscipline (41 percent, 16 percent, and 30 percent, respectively); however, response rate was considerably lower for this study, with only 66 percent, 59 percent, and 63 percent of the total number of each subdiscipline departments returning surveys, so Ammons's results should be considered more representative. Table 5.1 summarizes these findings.

Table 5.1
Percentage of U.S. Medical Schools with Live-Animal Laboratory Exercises in Various Departments

Department	Survey			
	OTA[a] (1985)	Barnard et al. (1988)	Ammons (1994)	Wolfe (1994)
Physiology	62.5 (n = 16)	53 (n = 93)	40 (n = 125)	41 (n = 83)
Pharmacology	50 (n = 16)	25 (n = 110)	10 (n = 125)	16 (n = 74)
Surgery	62.5 (n = 16)	19 (n = 81)	17 (n = 125)	30 (n = 80)

[a] Office of Technology Assessment

It is not necessary that surgeons must first train on animals before graduating to humans. Of those medical schools still using animals, all but one (the military's Uniformed Services University of the Health Sciences, in Maryland) present the terminal dog lab as an optional exercise. Still, the dog lab is used by about half of the 126 medical schools in the United States (Physicians Committee for Responsible Medicine 1997) and, where the lab is in place, students report that they are under considerable pressure to take it. Arluke and Hafferty (1996) concluded from their study of students at a Midwest American medical school that "the medical school culture provided absolutions to students that neutralized their moral apprehension about dog lab."

Though studies are few, the dog lab would not appear to have any pedagogical advantage over alternatives developed to replace it. In a study involving 110 medical students, both computer demonstrations and animal (dog) demonstrations were used and the former was rated higher by the students for learning cardiovascular physiology (Samsel et al. 1994). A study by Carpenter et al. (1991) documented equivalent training outcomes in medical students using cadaverized dogs compared with students using living, anaesthetized dogs, though both of these approaches are ethically charged.

Having students watch doctors performing operations in place of dog labs is becoming more common in American medical schools. Dr. Michael D'Ambra, who heads the Harvard Medical School's operating room program, believes that "the only thing a student can do in a dog lab that we don't cover in the operating room is killing the animal after the observation process is over" (McNaught 1998).

Regulations for the use of animals in medical training are stricter in Great Britain, where the apprenticeship approach to surgical training has been used for decades (Stephens 1986; Morton 1987). Under the Animals (Scientific Procedures) Act of 1986, use of animals for microsurgery training is now permitted, but only if the following conditions are met: the express consent of the Secretary of State must be obtained, the licensee must show that he/she is likely to be using microsurgery in his/her professional work, and only rats under full terminal anesthesia may be used (Morton 1987). Furthermore, use of decerebrate animals for training, which was outside the scope of the 1876 law, is prohibited by the 1986 law (ibid).

There is no question that hands-on surgical training improves surgical skills. The challenge for the future is how to provide the practical training without harming either human patients or animals. Perhaps computer-generated virtual reality will provide that answer.

Clinical Case-based Learning

The most important alternative to animal labs in medical training is the clinical apprenticeship teaching paradigm. The student trains in the true patient setting, being gradually given more responsibility and involvement as student competency improves. This case-based approach is the standard in Great Britain. The traditions of internship and residency in the United States are also examples of the apprenticeship training paradigm. This portion of medical training places the student in the real-life situations he/she will encounter as a professional practitioner.

Existing data show that case-based learning is favored by medical students. Lavine (1993) surveyed medical students at George Washington University, who in turn rated clinical case-based learning higher than laboratory sessions, basic lectures, and textbooks. By contrast, traditional terminal dog labs engender considerable worry and soul-searching for many medical students. Arluke and Hafferty (1996) found that medical students learn to use moral "absolutions," or reassurances, to cope with these feelings about dog labs.

Another valuable use of humans in medical training is the use of newly deceased patients to teach resuscitation procedures (Burns et al. 1994). A 1992 survey by Burns et al. (1994) found that 63 percent of U.S. emergency medicine programs and 58 percent of neonatal critical care programs allowed procedures to be performed on patients after their death. Tracheal intubation was by far the most commonly practiced procedure, but at least seven other procedures were also practiced. Postautopsy and prosected cadavers are a valuable resource for teaching surgical psychomotor skills and human anatomy (Jones et al. 1978; Morton 1987; Peterson 1993).

One of the drawbacks of clinical case-based experiences is that mistakes are costly and could endanger human life. This is where clinical simulations are invaluable. To supplement clinical-based training, simulations of case-based medicine are gaining ground as computer technology continues to improve. The University of Florida's $60 million brain institute includes a computer-driven patient simulator. Students use the simulator in emergency room drills, among other uses.

Other Alternatives

Beyond the clinical realm, the quality of replacement alternatives for medical training is already high and their availability is growing fast. Alternatives include human patient simulators (Stephanovsky 1998) and computerized mannequins (McCaffrey 1995), surgical and microsurgical training boards (Van Dongen et al. 1996), perfusion models, laparoscopy simulators (Tsang et al. 1994), and a wide range of computer platforms for learning anatomy, physiology (cardiovascular, pulmonary, renal, etc.), and gastrointestinal and muscle function (Carlson 1995). Virtual reality (VR), a developing technology with enormous future potential in the medical profession, is already making inroads into medical training (Coppa and Nachbar 1997; Thanki 1998). Alternatives have also been developed for advanced training in medical specialties, such as eye surgery (Hale 1989; Sinclair et al. 1995), and advanced trauma life support (ATLS).

Stephanovsky (1998) describes the success with which a new learning tool called the Human Patient Simulator (HPS) is being incorporated into the training of nurses, emergency medical services personnel, military personnel, and others. The HPS uses the principle of some of its veterinary predecessors (e.g., Resusci-Dog™, Resusci-Cat™) to create a lifelike mannequin that presents various vital signs and allows for a variety of manipulations. Among the features of this model are breathing and heart beat (normal and abnormal); palpable radial and carotid pulses; anatomy suitable for intubations and inductions; central venous, arterial and pulmonary arterial pressures; pulmonary capillary wedge pressures; oxygen saturation; and urinary catheterization (both male and female). HPS also allows students to administer over sixty different medications through three intravenous access sites (femoral, radial, and central) to which the "patient" then reacts according to patient profile, diagnosis, and amount delivered. Different monitors can be installed into the mannequin to provide diverse training experiences. One of the more simple yet innovative features of HPS is the speaker implanted into the throat area, allowing the instructor or another student, wearing a wireless microphone, to make it sound as if the patient is speaking; this provides valuable experience with the acquisition of patient assessment and bedside manner skills. These features allow students to track the patient as a complete case history from start to finish (Stephanovsky 1998).

Another example of innovation is the POP-Trainer (POP = perfused organ preparation), a simple but highly realistic apparatus for simulating operations. Waste slaughterhouse organs are perfused with a blood substitute in a closed system and operations are performed while the POP-Trainer pumps the fluid through the vessels in a lifelike manner. Other equipment from ultrasound to laser can be added. This device won the 1993 Felix Wankel Animal Protection Research Prize. Provided slaughterhouse materials are relinquished free of charge, The HSUS does not disapprove of making use of their availability for advanced training of this sort.

For the development of surgical skill, Reid and Vestrup (1986) credit models and simulations as being the best way to develop surgical skill and improve confidence prior to patient contact. Dennis (1999) surveys some of the inanimate surgery training models being used in veterinary and medical training programs. His conclusion is that currently, optimum training combines the use of both inanimate trainers and living animals, and that inanimate training aids, by themselves, can be as good as, or superior to, live-animal training methods.

Sophisticated and expensive equipment is not a prerequisite of effective surgical skills training. At the University of Pittsburgh, lacerated foliage leaves have been used for the introduction and refinement of microvascular suturing skills. Because the fragility of plant tissue (as compared with human tissue) exaggerates any damage done due to errors in technique, the use of plant tissue may enhance the trainees' acquisition of skills (Kaufman et al. 1984). At Erasmus University Medical School, in the Netherlands, frogs and rats were replaced with bicycle inner tubes and fig leaves in surgical training (Will Kort, personal communication, 1994). For microsurgery training, a range of options exists, including human placentas (McGregor 1980; Townsend 1985), inexpensive training cards (Awwad 1984), and a rat model for developing microsurgical skill, which was recently developed in the

Netherlands (van Dongen et al. 1996). Newsome et al. (1993) describe the replacement of live animals with tissues isolated from human and animal cadavers for use in laser surgery training and the reduction in animal use and in costs that accrued.

Exposure to real surgery in the operating room theater is obviously a vital component of surgical training (Morton 1987). As well as discarding its terminal dog surgery labs, Harvard University has begun sending its students to Massachusetts General, Beth Israel, and Brigham and Women's Hospitals, where they observe and study surgical procedures in the operating room (McNaught 1998). Observing operating room procedures helps medical students understand what it takes to apply medicine to real-world situations that help save and improve human lives.

Computer-based learning materials allow medical students, like their counterparts in other science fields, to work at their own pace and control various parameters in the experiment so that different effects can be observed. The computer-based experiment can also be repeated, an option rarely available in the animal experiment. Combining these resources is a way to further the benefits of each. Stanford et al. (1994) found that computer simulations used in conjunction with a dissection (of the human heart) enhanced learning compared with either computer training alone or the dissection alone.

Veterinary School

Veterinarians take an oath that includes the alleviation of animal suffering. Yet the invasive use of healthy animals in no need of medical intervention is widespread in U.S. veterinary schools. A census of all 27 U.S. veterinary schools conducted by the Office of Technology Assessment (OTA) in 1983-1984 estimated that 16,655 animals were being used yearly at that time, the most commonly used species being dogs (>8,000), mice (>2,000), rats (>2,000), and birds (>1,300). Uses include training in surgical techniques and dissection of animal cadavers. In most of these cases, the animals are dead or anesthetized at the time of use.

Veterinary schools in the United States are following the trend away from consumptive uses of healthy animals in their training programs. Anecdotal evidence indicates that animal use has declined since the OTA study in 1983-1984. Most of the veterinary schools in both the United States and Canada now have alternative tracks available for students who wish to minimize such contact with animals in their training. Many students report feeling pressure to do the traditional labs for fear that they may otherwise be less competent and/or may not be hired into the professional ranks. However, White et al. (1992) found that of three graduating veterinary students who had taken the alternative track in the Washington State University veterinary program, all received job offers, and two of them were hired because of (not in spite of) their participation in the alternatives program.

Harmful uses of animals has, for several years now, been eliminated in all six British veterinary colleges (Knight 1999).

The allied field of veterinary technology, whose graduates typically work as assistants in veterinary hospitals, also uses many animals to practice invasive, potentially painful procedures. A list of "essential" procedures for accreditation by the American Veterinary Medical Association (1998) for training technicians includes tail docking, and the dehorning of cattle and goats. A veterinary technology student at the University of Cincinnati complained to The HSUS in 1997 that students with little or no prior training were required to perform oral dosing of rats (in which four of the animals died); intraperitoneal and intramuscular injections of mice, rats and rabbits; and jugular blood drawing from dogs. Veterinary technicians on the job must often perform many blood drawings daily. But a more sensible and humane approach would involve students working with lifelike prosthetic models (see next paragraph), then working with live animals under close supervision in the clinical setting, rather than using purpose-bred rodents.

Alternatives for Veterinary Training

Nonanimal surgical training devices are used extensively in veterinary schools to help students hone skills prior to their application to live-animal tissue. Anatomical models, for example, have proven effective in the training of veterinary skills and techniques (Johnson and Farmer 1989; Greenfield et al. 1993, 1995; Holmberg et al. 1993; Holmberg and Cockshutt 1994). Soft-tissue plastic models of canine abdominal organs developed at the University of Illinois were found to have comparable handling properties and were useful for teaching a range of common surgical procedures (Greenfield et al. 1993). The Scottish-based company Moredun (n.d.) produces simulators for practicing a variety of common procedures done by veterinarians or their assistants, including a mouse tail that forms a hematoma if poorly handled during "blood" drawing.

The DASIE (Dog Abdominal Surrogate for Instructional Exercises), developed at the Ontario Veterinary College, has also been successfully used to prepare students for live surgery (Holmberg et al. 1993; Holmberg and Cockshutt 1994). More rigid plastics have been used to make bone models, and these have been used effectively for demonstrating and teaching many aspects of bone-related surgical procedures (DeYoung and Richardson 1987; Johnson et al. 1990). Of twenty-seven respondents to a survey of all thirty-one veterinary schools in the United States and Canada, Bauer (1993) reported that plastic bones were being used in eight schools (30 percent) to teach fracture repair. A model of a dog stomach developed and tested at Ohio State University by Smeak et al. (1994) had mixed results; it was effective for teaching some procedures but was not found to enhance the confidence of students faced with live-animal surgery, suggesting that accompanying instruction was necessary. Table 5.2 presents studies of alternative methods and approaches in veterinary education.

Table 5.2
Studies Evaluating Alternatives in Veterinary Medical Education

Authors	Study Subjects	Principal Findings
Carpenter et al. 1991	24 third-year veterinary students	No significant differences were detected between the surgical performance of two groups, one trained using live animals, the other using cadavers (source unknown).
Erickson and Clegg 1993	82 U.S. veterinary students	Of 14 learning methods for basic cardiac teaching and ECG interpretation, computer-based active learning was rated the highest in student evaluations.
Fawver et al. 1990	85 first-year U.S. veterinary students	Use of interactive videodisc simulations yielded equivalent test performance and greater time efficiency in teaching cardiovascular physiology compared with instruction in a live-animal laboratory.
Greenfield et al. 1995	36 third-year U.S. veterinary students	Surgical skills were evaluated following training with dogs and cats, or soft-tissue organ models; performance of each group was equivalent.
Johnson and Farmer 1989	100 U.S. veterinary students	Inanimate models effectively taught basic psychomotor skills and had the advantage over live animals that they could be used repeatedly, enhancing the acquisition of motor proficiency.
Pavletic et al. 1994	48 U.S. veterinary graduates	No difference was found in surgical confidence or ability of graduates who had participated in an alternatives course of study versus those who had participated in a conventional course of study.
Sandquist 1991	373 U.S. veterinary students	51 percent of students felt that alternatives to surgery labs should be available to students unwilling to participate in terminal surgeries.
White et al. 1992	7 fourth-year alternative track veterinary students	After hesitancy in their first live-tissue surgery, students from an alternative surgical laboratory program performed on par with students with a standard laboratory experience.

The technology of VR also has applications to veterinary education. The School of Veterinary Medicine at Michigan State University, for example, is currently establishing a curriculum that relies heavily on VR. Endotracheal intubation, ovariohysterectomy and castration, intravenous catheterization, and venipuncture are some of the procedures being transformed into VR technology (Thanki 1998). A unique advantage of VR over traditional surgical training methods is that virtual images can be enlarged, even to the point of allowing the student to "walk" around inside the abdominal cavity of a dog.

Suturing is a vital but basic skill that can be easily simulated without having to use live or dead animals. Not surprisingly, even relatively simple synthetic suture simulators have been shown to improve veterinary surgical skills over merely observing suture technique (Smeak et al. 1991). Bauer and Seim (1992) describe two inanimate models—the fluid homeostasis model and the interactive electronic suturing board—developed at Colorado State University that can be used for both teaching and objective evaluation. Among the many advantages of these nonanimal surgery training devices are that they are inexpensive, they allow repeated use at the student's convenience without the need for aseptic surroundings, and they are not ethically problematic. They help improve proficiency so that subsequent experiences with surgery on animals will be more rewarding and more likely to bolster confidence.

Learning in the Clinical Setting

Increasingly, veterinary schools are using animals in the clinical setting to help train their students. A fast-growing practice is the spay/neuter of cats and dogs from local shelters. Bauer (1993) reported that 16 of 27 North American veterinary schools (59 percent) had implemented some type of program with local humane societies. Among the schools now using this approach are Ohio State University (Smeak 1998), Tufts University (Patronek 1998), Kansas State University (Roush 1998), Mississippi State University (Bushby 1997), and Colorado State University (Jones and Borchert 1999). This is a win-win-win situation for the school (which gains access to a low-cost source of animals for surgical training), the shelter (which receives virtually free spay/neuter services), and the animals (who are more likely to be adopted afterward). One of the distinct advantages of this approach, as compared with performing terminal surgeries on animals, is that it gives students exposure to all phases of patient care, including postsurgical pain management. As Brown et al. (1993) report, programs for teaching that involve surgery on animals should include perioperative experiences; that is, they should involve all aspects of preoperative, operative, and postoperative experience.

Tufts University's anatomy and medical skills programs recently achieved the goal of using only cadavers donated by clinic clients whose companion animals had died a natural death or were euthanized for medical reasons (Patronek 1998). The main surgery courses now use shelter animals who are later returned to the shelter for adoption. Tufts also offers field experience in surgery and shelter medicine through externships to animal shelters, a Native American reservation in Nevada, and a one- to two-week summer feral cat sterilization project in one of the Virgin Islands (ibid.).

Veterinary students also can and should gain valuable surgical training in the operating room under the close supervision of an experienced surgical instructor/practitioner (Johnson et al. 1990). Here, the student mostly observes at first, performing relatively simple procedures like incision making and suturing; as competence and exposure develop, the student takes on more complex surgical tasks.

Bauer et al. (1992a, b) describe curricular changes made at Purdue University's veterinary school, which replaced use of two consecutive survival surgeries performed on purpose-bred cats and dogs with a greater emphasis on clinical casework and use of animals from local animal shelters (both cadavers and live animals for spay/neuter surgery). The authors found that students' motivation, attitude, and self-confidence remained undiminished following these changes (Bauer et al. 1992b), and that the new approach also yielded budgetary and social benefits (Bauer et al. 1992a). The use of animal cadavers has also been found to be as instructive as the terminal use of living dogs for training veterinary students in surgery techniques (Carpenter et al. 1991; Pavletic et al. 1994). White et al. (1992) found that students who had studied surgery using cadavers were more timid and hesitant during their first surgery on a live animal, but thereafter, these students performed on par with other students on this and all other segments of the surgery and anesthesia rotations. Ten veterinary students at Kansas State University showed superior surgical skills after repeatedly conducting survival surgeries on animals who were returned to a local shelter for adoption (the "new" curriculum) than did students who performed a number of terminal surgeries (the "old" curriculum) (Fingland 1999).

Nedim Buyukmihci, a veterinarian with the School of Veterinary Medicine at the University of California–Davis, has proposed the use of terminally ill companion animals for surgical training. The animal's guardian would sign a consent form, the patient would be deeply anesthetized, then the various training procedures would be done before the animal was killed via overdose without recovering consciousness (Buyukmihci 1995).

It is important to note that the surgical training that students receive at veterinary school does not make them proficient surgeons. Logistics, costs, and time constraints require that the amount of hands-on surgical experience is limited. It is not until veterinarians apply the lessons learned through repeated practice on the job that they begin to attain high levels of surgical competence and skill.

For students seeking instruction in laboratory animal handling techniques, Duffy (1999) summarizes examples of positive applications of various alternative methods. These include simulation models (for restraint and handling, venipuncture, endotracheal intubation, and surgical technique) and computer media, including virtual reality CD-ROMs now available from the School of Veterinary Medicine at the University of California–Davis. Innovative models of both the rat and the rabbit have been developed by the Japanese company Koken. The Koken Rat, a realistic model of a nineteen-week-old male laboratory rat, allows lab technicians, veterinary students, and others to learn proper methods of handling, dosing, injecting, intubating, and drawing blood. These models are now in use in many institutions around the world (EuroNICHE 1999). Resusci-Dog and Resusci-Cat are also widely used for training veterinary technologists and other allied professionals in emergency treatment and life support for companion animals. Rescue Critters, a new line of animal mannequins for the training of veterinary and veterinary support staff, are now in use at twenty-three U.S. colleges as well as five overseas schools, and over 200 chapters of the American Red Cross's Pet First Aid classes (Craig Jones, personal communication, 25 October 1999).

Training in animal welfare issues is also improving, with at least seven U.S. veterinary schools now offering such courses (Self et al. 1994; Balcombe 1999). British veterinary schools (with one exception) provide a required course devoted to animal welfare (Stewart 1989), wherein students are taught all the factors that contribute to animal health and well-being and learn to identify signs of pain and distress and suffering in different species of animals (ibid.).

For certain skills, live-animal use is beneficial, even indispensable, to the training of veterinarians. It does not follow, however, that healthy animals need be harmed to obtain such skills. Just as students in the field of human medicine can be trained to be excellent, life-saving practitioners without ever killing or deliberately harming another human being, veterinary students ought to be able to do the same without harming or killing animals.

5.5 Science Fairs

Because they fall somewhat outside the purview of sanctioned classroom animal use, and because they may involve more ambitious scientific explorations than typically occur in the classroom, science fairs have more potential to include invasive use of live animals than any other facet of precollege education. The history of science fairs over the past several decades contains many examples of students being awarded prizes for science fair projects that involve harming and killing animals (Orlans 1993), and more harmful projects that receive no prizes. Though one million American students participate in mostly local science fairs yearly, much of what is known of animal use is from the two major science fair competitions in the United States: the International Science and Engineering Fair (ISEF), and the Intel Science Talent Search (ISTS, formerly the Westinghouse Science Talent Search, WSTS). Both of these science fairs are now funded by the Intel Corporation.

The WSTS began prohibiting invasive studies of vertebrates in 1969, in response to protest over a student's prizewinning project that involved blinding sparrows that subsequently starved (blind birds will not move). The ISEF, in contrast, has continued to permit and even encourage invasive projects and has actively resisted attempts to prohibit such studies (Orlans 1993). A 1985 survey of ISEF projects found that when vertebrate animals were used, four of five projects involved harming the animals (Orlans 1988a). Twenty of the winning projects from ISEF's 1985 and 1986 competitions involved demonstrations of the harmful effects of well-known toxic substances (ibid.). The 1999 ISEF included projects that had teenagers injecting animals with cancer cells, nicotine, high doses of antibiotics, or amphetamines, or exposing them to radiation (Opinion Research Corp. 1999). The permissiveness of this science fair sets an unfortunate example to lesser fairs.

Public sentiment disfavors the current status of animal use in science fairs. In a 1999 survey of 1,000 American adults, 79 percent disapproved of student science fair experiments that are harmful or painful to the animals, and 78 percent believed that science fair rules should be changed to prohibit such experiments (ORC 1999). Yet, as Morton (1987) observes, ISEF's regulations appear to constitute poorer oversight of students than that required of scientists by the Animal Welfare Act.

Efforts by animal protection groups and/or concerned scientists to strengthen humane guidelines for science fairs continue. Orlans (1993) believes that secondary school students should not be permitted to inflict pain or a lingering death on vertebrate animals and that judgment of what may be appropriate use of animals should be left to students' supervisors and IACUCs. For more than twenty years, the Women's Humane Society, based in Bensalem, Pennsylvania, has been awarding "Humane Awards" for science fair projects that treat animals humanely, find alternatives to animal-based methods of research, and/or directly benefit animals. In 1998 this organization also presented its first "Humane Award" at the fiftieth ISEF, in Philadelphia.

5.6 HSUS Recommendations

1. School exercises that involve killing, undernourishing, or otherwise harming live animals should be replaced with humane alternatives, such as computer simulations, observational and behavioral field study, and benign investigations of the students themselves.

2. The traditional frog and turtle pithing exercises should be terminated and replaced with computer packages, which have been shown to save time and money without compromising educational value. Studies that involve the students as investigators and subjects should be more widely adopted.

3. Medical schools still using live terminal dog labs should follow the lead of other schools that have replaced these procedures with labs that employ a clinical approach with human patients.

4. Veterinary schools should accelerate the current trend towards replacement of purpose-bred and/or healthy animals with clinical cases for surgical training, including spay/neuter of shelter animals.

5. Recognizing that perioperative experience, including handling live tissue, is a critical part of a veterinary education, student participation in actual clinical cases coupled with primary surgical experience performing procedures of benefit to the animal (e.g., spay/neuter of shelter animals) should wholly replace traditional "survival" surgeries.

6. For common surgeries that are not medically required by an individual animal, only two options should exist: (1) terminal surgery on anesthetized, terminally ill animals with guardian consent or (2) cadaver surgery where cadavers are ethically obtained.

7. All science fairs should abide by a policy against inflicting deliberate harm on sentient animals.

8. Laws should be implemented that require a certain level of competency before a person is allowed to conduct animal experiments.

[1]The IACUC granted full approval for these labs, and The HSUS filed a complaint with the university. Subsequent negotiations resulted in termination of the rabbit lab and a number of refinements being made to the mouse labs. The university's IACUC chair and staff veterinarian showed considerable concern and willingness to work with The HSUS, but the persistence of the main portion of animal use in this course (the mice labs) illustrates the difficulties faced by a university in changing a tenured faculty member's choice of teaching method. Naturally, there is a reluctance to criticize one's peer, who is no doubt quite genuine in his/her belief that his/her personal choices of method are made with the highest educational goals in mind.

Law and Policy Issues

I just don't think we should be playing God. Dissection doesn't help us or the animal. It doesn't benefit medical science, and the animals are just thrown away like trash when it's over.

—Melissa Chodan,
fourteen, New Jersey student

Children should be given a choice between dissection or using a computer program. That will be done here now because of Melissa's dedication and love for animals.

—Laura Morana,
Melissa's school principal

6.1 Introduction

From a policy standpoint, the dissection issue is one of conflicting rights. It pits the right of the student to learn using methods that are not inimical to his/her ethical beliefs against the right of the school to require the student to learn solely by the methods it decrees. One way to resolve such a conflict is to analyze relative costs and benefits to the claimants of those rights. The analysis presented in the first part of this chapter weighs clearly on the side of the student. Following this, a condensed summary of recent legal challenges mounted by student conscientious objectors against school dissection requirements is presented. Reviewed next are current laws and policies, their strengths and weaknesses, and evidence that their enforcement is poor. Finally, the elements of a good policy are discussed, and recommendations made for their adoption nationwide.

6.2 The Case for Student Choice

A major focus of the dissection debate has been on student choice: specifically, do students have the right to choose a method of learning? As the numbers of students who object to dissection have grown (Mayer and Hinton 1990; Gilmore 1991b; Orlans 1992; Solot 1995), so, too, have efforts to make student choice a legal mandate, and seven states now have laws or policies upholding a student's right to choose (table 6.1).

Table 6.1
U.S. State Student Choice-in-Dissection Laws

Provisions	Florida	California	Maine[a]	Louisiana[b]
Year enacted	1985	1988	1989	1992
Grade range	K-12	K-12	K-12	K-12
Private schools	exempt	exempt	not mentioned	Parish school system non-exempt
Notification of student	parent/guardian only	parent/guardian and student	student	student
Written consent	required from parent/guardian	required from parent/guardian	not mentioned	not mentioned
Penalty for objecting	not mentioned	no penalty	no penalty	no penalty
Alternative testing[c]	not mentioned	yes	yes	yes
Teacher discretion to overrule	no	yes	no	no
Definition of "animal"	unclear: may be only mammals and birds	vertebrates and invertebrates	vertebrates and invertebrates	animals (mammals?), reptiles, or amphibians
Experiments on living animals	no surgery on mammals and birds; otherwise, no physiological harm	prohibited under separate Education Code 51540	prohibited in public and private schools under separate law (3971)	none explicitly prohibited

Provisions	Pennsylvania	New York	Rhode Island
Year enacted	1992	1994	1997
Grade range	K-12	K-12 (implied)	K-12
Private schools	non-exempt	exempt	non-exempt
Notification of student	parent/guardian and student	none required	not mentioned
Written consent	not mentioned	required from parent/guardian	not mentioned
Penalty for objecting	no penalty	no penalty	no penalty
Alternative testing	yes	not mentioned	not mentioned
Teacher discretion to overrule	no	yes (for 10th to 12th grade)	no
Definition of "animal"	vertebrates only	unclear: may be only mammals and birds	vertebrates and invertebrates
Experiments on living animals	none explicitly prohibited	16 procedures listed as prohibited (e.g., surgery, electric shock)	none explicitly prohibited

[a] Bill did not pass in Maine, but was voluntarily adopted by the Maine Department of Education.
[b] Passed as a state resolution.
[c] School should also offer alternative means of testing students' knowledge.

Note: In 1997 both Maryland and Illinois enacted a law requiring school boards to publish information on availability of, and student access to, alternatives to dissection.

Not surprisingly, students almost universally support a student's right to choose alternatives to dissection (see table 3.1), and this includes students who themselves have no personal aversion or objection to dissection (Brown 1989; McKernan 1991; Bennett 1994). Both the American Medical Student Association (1993) and the National Student Nurses Association (1997) have issued position statements in support of student choice regarding animal dissection. In spring 1998 Cornell University's Undergraduate Student Assembly unanimously voted for a resolution supporting student choice (Pease 1998).

The American public also clearly favors student choice in dissection. In a recent poll (May 1999) of 1,000 randomly selected American adults, conducted by the National Anti–Vivisection Society, nearly 9 out of 10 people surveyed believed that high school students who object to dissection should be offered the choice of using other methods (ORC 1999).

Educators, on the other hand, are more inclined to feel that they should control the decision of whether students should dissect or not (Offner 1995; Schmidt 1999), though it is not clear whether or not a majority of teachers feel this way. A primary reason why student choice bills did not pass in both the Maryland and Massachusetts legislatures during the nineties was the successful lobbying against these measures by members of the science education establishment. The only parties that officially opposed passage of California's student choice-in-dissection bill in 1988 were science education associations (Legislative Research Inc. n.d.). Pat Davis (formerly Graham), who campaigned for this law with her daughter, Jenifer, believes that her school district's strict adherence to the dissection requirement had more to do with the perceived threat to its authority than with its concern about Jenifer's development as a student (personal communication, 16 June 1999).

Apparently, more than education and economic motives maintain the status quo. Because the educational establishment so values its right to academic freedom (Terry 1992), it is perhaps reluctant to recognize the right of student choice in dissection. Teachers who support and use dissection appear to view objecting students as disruptive and rebellious. Snyder et al. (1992) urge teachers to watch out for students "parroting" animal rights literature, implying that a student's objection based on moral argument is disingenuous and insincere. But if the student has read and thought about the issues and has gone to the trouble—and assumed the risk—of voicing an objection to the teacher, then it seems proper to assume that the student is serious about the matter.

An educator's reluctance to accommodate a student may also be attributable to a fear that capitulation to one conscientious objector could open the floodgates to a deluge of other objecting students. Francione and Charlton (1992) report that the dean of students at Ohio State University (OSU) College of Veterinary Medicine expressed his fear that if student Jennifer Kissinger—who sued the school in 1990 for the right to use humane alternatives to labs that harmed healthy animals—were allowed to use alternatives, other students would demand to do the same.

It is also worth noting that teachers routinely accommodate students with special needs, such as the hearing or visually challenged. To do otherwise would be discriminatory and illegal. But, as Buyukmihci (1991) asks: why should it be any different for students who object to harming or killing nonhuman animals in the name of education? Balcombe (1997b) likens requiring dissection of a student who objects to the practice on moral grounds to requiring a vegetarian to eat meat as part of a nutrition course. Barnard and Baron (1989) draw upon the abortion debate to present a useful analogy for a student's right to decline on ethical grounds without penalty: no medical student would be required to perform an abortion if he/she objects to it.

Who has more to lose, students if they are not given a choice on dissection, or teachers if they are? Shapiro (1987) believes it is the student: "In commonsense terms, which violates the respective individual's rights more: if we force an individual (a student) to injure, harm, inflict pain on, or kill an animal when his or her conscience dictates otherwise; or if we force another individual (a teacher) merely to add a supplemental noninvasive procedure to the curriculum?"

The National Association of Biology Teachers (NABT 1995) has not taken a consistent stand on this matter over the past decade. In 1990 Rosalina Hairston, NABT's executive director, wrote that "teachers need not—indeed, should not—decide how they feel and then impose that opinion on their students. Instead, students should be given the opportunity to explore the issue themselves and come to their own conclusions" (Hairston 1990, 91). NABT's 1995 statement on dissection upheld this view of student self-determination (NABT 1995), but the current executive director, Wayne Carley, believes "that choice [in dissection] rests with a well-educated, experienced teacher" (Carley 1998).

In 1997 the NABT began screening materials from some organizations planning to exhibit at their conventions. Animal protection organizations that oppose dissection were a focus of this screening. NABT's explanation for this was to allow only "distribution of materials that do not contradict the association's stated policies and that do not slander, libel, or interfere with other exhibitors" (NABT 1999). In 1997 NABT rejected three of the sixteen items The HSUS submitted for approval. The American Anti–Vivisection Society had eleven of twenty-three items rejected in 1997 and eleven of twenty-five items rejected in 1998. The National Anti–Vivisection Society (operators of the NAVS Dissection Hotline) had seven of thirteen items rejected in 1998 and eight of sixteen items rejected in 1999.

Academic freedom is finite, and it has a counterpart: academic duty (Kennedy 1997). Frank Rhodes, president emeritus of Cornell University, says in his review of Kennedy: "If professors are unwilling to establish reasonable norms and standards for their own professional conduct and performance, others...will do so" (Rhodes 1997, 1726). It is fair to suggest that the influx of dissection choice laws in the United States would not have taken place had not teachers and/or school administrations resisted students who believe harming animals in schools is unethical.

6.3 Legal Challenges

When students object conscientiously to dissection assignments, their cases are usually resolved without any resort to legal action. Occasionally, however, a student has filed a lawsuit against her/his school, usually on grounds that the student's First Amendment rights (to freedom of religion) have been violated by a requirement that the student participate in an activity that she/he finds unethical (Francione and Charlton 1992). Legal case history in the United States indicates that the right of a student is usually upheld in cases of conscientious objection.

The most celebrated dissection lawsuit was filed in June 1987 by Jenifer Graham, a California high school student who was told by her school board to either dissect a frog or accept a lowered biology grade and negative evaluation on her school transcript. Ms. Graham's case marked the first time that a student had made a legal challenge to required dissection exercises. Nine months after the lawsuit was filed, then California governor George Deukmejian signed into law a bill requiring that elementary and secondary students be allowed to choose whether or not to dissect animals in science classes. In August 1988 Judge Manuel Real dismissed Ms. Graham's suit when the school agreed to reinstate her grade and to remove the notation from her transcript.

The case generated widespread publicity and set the stage for additional lawsuits and enactments of law. Maggie McCool, who refused to dissect a fetal pig, frog, and other animals in her New Jersey high school biology class, sued the school in 1989 for giving her a failing grade and declining to let her use alternatives. An out-of-court settlement required the school to recalculate Ms. McCool's grade without the dissection labs and required a statement in the student hand-book that students with religious objections to dissection be provided with alter-natives (Orlans 1993). Jennifer Kissinger, a third-year veterinary student at Ohio State University (OSU), sued her school in 1990 for refusing to allow her to use alternatives to labs that cause harm and death to healthy animals (Francione and Charlton 1992). Ms. Kissinger faced expulsion from OSU's veterinary program at the time she filed suit. She won her case and was provided with an alternative cur-riculum for which she used cadavers, then assisted with and later performed surgery on sick or injured animals (*PR Newswire* 1991). Safia Rubaii, a medical student at the University of Colorado, sued her school for not permitting her to use a humane alternative to its terminal dog lab. She left the school to complete her training elsewhere. The courts ruled in her favor and the school was ordered to pay her $95,000 (Romano 1995). Beate Broese-Quinn, a biology student at Foothills Community College, California, sued her school in 1998 for requiring her participation in a biology exam that used prosected (already dissected) fetal pigs. This case was pending as of early 2000.

Notwithstanding the tendency for courts to side with student conscientious objectors to dissection, it is probably in a school's better interest to accommodate such students, and most of them do. Many thousands of students request alterna-tives to dissection each year, and while many outcomes may be suboptimal, many others are resolved without problem for either the school/teacher or the student.

6.4 Current Laws and Policies

In spite of the evidence that dissection choice for conscientious objectors is constitutional, dissection choice laws and policies in the United States are more the exception than the rule. Since 1985, when Florida became the first state to enact a dissection choice law, seven states have implemented such laws (see table 6.1). Choice-in-dissection bills were introduced in the legislatures of New Hampshire, Illinois, Massachusetts, and New Jersey in the late nineties. In 1999 Illinois Governor George Ryan placed an amendatory veto on a student choice-in-dissection bill that had passed both state house and senate; the bill was expected to pass into law. This particular bill would have been precedent setting because it included not only kindergarten through secondary school but also post-secondary institutions. Nevertheless, such laws are not free of loopholes (Bal-combe 1996), and their implementation and enforcement depend on both the diligence of school superintendents (in informing their teachers), and teacher compliance.

Most American high schools and colleges continue to have no written policy for accommodating student objections to dissection. For example, of twenty-four county school boards in the state of Maryland, only one (Prince George's) has a written pol-icy prescribing choice in dissection for its students. Massachusetts and Connecticut are two of the stronger states; at least six school systems in Massachusetts (Kerstet-ter 1993), and forty-five schools in Connecticut have dissection choice policies. Chicago public schools implemented a policy in 1993 that provides student choice in dissection. There are others but they represent a small minority of the schools.

Gilmore (1991b) surveyed all public high schools in Connecticut, plus a few private schools. Of the eighty-one responding schools, 54 percent made dissection mandatory, 40 percent made it optional, and 6 percent gave no response to the question. In a teacher survey by the *American School Board Journal* (1992), 52 percent of respondents felt that dissection should be mandatory; 35 percent felt that it should be an optional activity. Thirteen percent supported abolishing dissection altogether. In a survey of 191 Canadian undergraduates, Bowd (1993) found that 69 percent had been required to perform dissections in secondary school.

The dearth of dissection-choice policies is unfortunate, for a good policy can benefit both student and teacher (Snyder et al. 1992). Students know their rights from the outset (Bekoff 1999), and potential problems are recognized early so that last-minute, seat-of-the-pants negotiating is avoided.

Dissection policies are also rare in postsecondary education, and those written policies that do exist are likely to consist of assertions that student participation is mandatory and students who do not wish to participate in a given course exercise should not enroll in the course. The HSUS maintains a list of schools with such policies. Nevertheless, universities have implemented student choice policies; one such policy, implemented by Sarah Lawrence College (Bronxville, New York) in 1994, reads as follows:

> Sarah Lawrence College does not require students with ethical objections to participate in dissection. Students who choose to refrain from such activities will be given alternatives that provide similar experiences. Those who choose such alternatives will not be penalized, although they will be responsible for the material presented in these exercises. If appropriate, separate evaluations of their learning experiences may be designed. In courses where dissection is considered to be fundamental and therefore mandatory, students should be informed of this during registration.
>
> Students who feel that undue pressure to dissect has been placed upon them, or question the designation of a course as requiring mandatory dissection, may file a complaint with the Dean of the College.

The advent of regulations governing animal research and testing has clearly been driven in part by public protest against the use of animals in these endeavors. By comparison, the level of protest against animal use in education has been substantially lower. This is perhaps because the use of animals in education has not been perceived by the public as being as serious an issue.

6.5 International Policy

In most of the world, animal-use practices in education go unreported and laws or policies explicitly referring to such use do not exist. There are notable exceptions, however, particularly in Europe, where the fourteen nations of the European Union (EU) prohibit invasive uses of live animals in primary and secondary schools (Orlans 1995). Animal dissection has been banned in at least three countries: Argentina in 1987 (Stuart 1988), the Slovak Republic in 1994 (*The Animals' Agenda,* July/August 1994, 7), and Israel in 1999. In 1993 the Italian parliament passed a law that grants the right of any citizen to refuse to participate in any form of animal experimentation without penalty.

In the United Kingdom, the Animals (Scientific Procedures) Act of 1986 specifically prohibits the use of animals in primary and secondary schools where that animal can be expected to suffer adverse effects (Morton 1987). Whole-animal dissection is no longer required by any of the U.K. examining boards (Reiss 1993), though a survey of English secondary school teachers in charge of biological science by Adkins and Lock (1994) showed extensive use of live and dead animals in the classroom. In Holland, dissection and live-animal experimentation in precollege education are prohibited by law, and the Experiments on Animals Act in the Netherlands forbids animal experiments if alternatives can yield equivalent results (Nab 1989).

Legislation adopted in the EU in the mid-eighties asserted that animal use for education and training is not appropriate for secondary schools; that it should be used only for students aiming to be professional scientists; and that alternatives must first be considered and found unsuitable as replacements (Morton 1987). Article 26 of the European Directive requires that persons carrying out, taking part in, or caring for animals used in live-animal use procedures—such as technicians and biomedical scientists—shall have had appropriate education and training (De Greeve 1989; van Zutphen 1989). Unfortunately, however, training requirements for animal technicians and researchers vary considerably among European countries (van Zutphen et al. 1989).

As a result of a student protest, Murdoch University, in Western Australia, adopted a university–wide policy in November 1998, formally allowing conscientious objection and agreeing to review humane alternatives for all teaching units that use animals (Knight 1998). As part of his argument against the school, veterinary student Andrew Knight cited Article 18 of the Universal Declaration of Human Rights, proclaimed by the United Nations General Assembly (1948): "Everyone has the right to freedom of thought, conscience, and religion; this right includes freedom to change his religion or belief, and freedom, either alone or in community with others and in public or private, to manifest his religion or belief in teaching, practice, worship and observance."

The continents of Asia, Africa, and South America are largely unknowns when it comes both to the practices and policies regarding animal use in education. China, for example, has no controls, no laws, and no reporting of animal use in its schools (Balcombe, *Animal Use in Higher Education,* in press).

India, by contrast, has shown signs of substantial change in its use of animals in education. In May 1997, the Ministry for Human Resource Development of the Government of India told the Delhi High Court that it had decided to make dissection optional for school students, and this decision was implemented in the spring of 1998. In May 1998 the state of Rajasthan banned the dissection of frogs in its schools in response to a campaign by Mahajanam, a group advocating nonviolence (Abdi 1998).

6.6 Enforcement Problems

Although laws and policies that allow students to use alternatives instead of harmful exercises are an improvement over no guidance at all, problems with implementation and enforcement remain. Teachers and students should be aware of such laws and policies, but what information there is suggests that students, especially, lack such awareness.

McKernan (1991) reported that only one-third of approximately 1,450 students she surveyed knew that they could request an alternative to dissection. Rosenthal (1994) reported that in many cases neither students nor parents received notification of their right to refuse to dissect in Pennsylvania, where a dissection-choice law was enacted in 1993. In a survey of 373 American veterinary students, 58 percent responded that they were not sure whether or not their school had a policy for students refusing to participate in student surgery (Sandquist 1991). The HSUS continues to receive complaints from students residing in states with dissection-choice laws; in some cases neither students nor the teacher is aware of the law's existence.

Most students unaware that they may have a choice in whether or not to participate in a dissection exercise will usually dissect without openly objecting. Today, most teachers would probably accommodate a student who requests an alternative to an animal dissection assignment, but few students desire to openly question their teacher's method. As Mayer and Hinton (1990) reported: "It should be no surprise that nearly every [teacher] using dissection felt that it was a very effective teaching tool." Students know this, and it stifles objection.

6.7 What Constitutes a Good Policy

No two dissection policies are the same. They represent a diversity of elements and styles. For policies to be effective and fair, they must contain some elements. For precollege these are:

- Students are notified of the policy verbally and in writing prior to the start of the course
- There is no penalty for objecting conscientiously
- Alternative assignments involve a comparable amount of work
- Available alternatives cover the same basic information as does the dissection and do not merely provide a comparable amount of effort from the student
- Student conscientious objectors are tested in ways that do not harm animals
- Teachers engage their students in a discussion of the pros/cons of dissection, and students should be encouraged to express their personal viewpoints without censure
- Teachers should not be required to use dissection in the teaching of anatomy

State laws should define "animal" broadly to accommodate students who do not want to harm the animal, regardless of whether the animal in question is sentient or not. The question of where one draws the line of sentiency is unclear (Regan 1983), and it is better to err on the side of caution. The policy should apply to all animals believed capable of feeling pain or distress (this includes all vertebrates).

Finally, watching other students dissect should never be viewed as an acceptable alternative to dissection. Based on the number of complaints received by The HSUS, it is very commonplace for teachers to instruct conscientiously objecting students that they may just observe the dissection. This perceived solution suggests that the teacher assumes the student objects for reasons of squeamishness. But for students with moral objections to the practice, watching is not an acceptable practice. Only 25 percent of the respondents in a survey of 468 British high school students felt that watching other people dissect was acceptable (Lock and Millett 1991).

6.8 Recommendations

1. *All* students should have a legally mandated right to use humane alternatives to dissection and other classroom exercises harmful to animals. Currently, less than one in five American states have statewide laws or policies mandating student choice in dissection, with the result that some students are granted rights that others are denied. States still lacking such laws should make their enactment a high priority.
2. Dissection-choice laws should apply to students at all levels of education; currently, such laws apply only to precollege students and exclude postsecondary students, even though the validity of conscientious objection is independent of learning level.
3. IACUCs should apply more stringent restrictions on proposals for animal use in instruction and should always look for ways to piggyback teaching exercises that involve animals in ongoing research at the institution.

Conclusion

Wee, sleekit, tim'rous, cowrin beastie,
Oh, what a panic's in thy breastie,
Thy need not start away so hastie
With bickering brattle,
I would be loathe to run and chase thee
With murd'ring pattle.

—Robert Burns

Despite recent advances in technology and increasing societal concern for animals, animals continue to be exploited and killed in large numbers so that students can learn about their structure and function. Dissection may not be without its merits from an educational standpoint, if well implemented, but it appears from student surveys that it usually is not. When one considers the associated costs—animal suffering and death in the supply trade, disruption of wild animal populations, messages that tend to undermine rather than reinforce respect for life and concern for others, rising costs of animal carcasses (as compared with alternatives with longer shelf lives), exposure to potentially harmful chemicals, and greater time expenditures in preparing and presenting various animal-based exercises—the balance clearly falls on the side of abandoning dissection, at least in its current form.

One possible reason for dissection's continued prominence in life science education is tradition. Today's biology teachers, science administrators, legislators, and parents were taught using animal dissections. Dissection is a familiar, comfortable, tried-and-true teaching method.

Dissection has a veneer of "real science" to it. Because it involves once-living animals, it gives the illusion that it is that much closer than a simulation to real-world, "cutting-edge" science. This impression is commonly conveyed in the comments of students who have participated in dissections (e.g., Solot 1995; Barr, in press). But while careful observation is an important part of a scientist's vocation, the dissection exercise is devoid of the hypothesis testing that defines the scientific process.

Dissection persists because it is a readily available way for a teacher to bring a student closer to a once-living organism. Who can fault a teacher for wanting to do that?

If an educator feels that student contact with the internal structures of once-living animals is essential, then he/she should seek out ethical sources of animal (or human) cadavers. If an educator views anatomy and physiology as an essential part of the curriculum, then he/she has an enormous range of proven materials—from computer simulations to student self-study modules—from which to choose. But if the educator wants to teach both the life and the science that comprise the life science discipline, then he/she will provide students with opportunities to do inquiry-based, scientific studies of living organisms. Students will be given the chance to ask questions about life that are meaningful to them. They will learn how to conduct a scientific experiment from start to finish—not by merely being told how it is done, but by doing it themselves, with guidance and encouragement.

This, of course, is not a revolutionary idea. The National Science Education Standards are unequivocal in their support of inquiry-based learning, and many teachers are using a variety of creative life science learning modules that emphasize learning by doing (see chapter 2). But for the most part, life science education today remains mired in the textbook, the lecture, and the "cookbook" lab, and in the morbid study of dead or dying organisms. The time has come to unite inquiry-based, active learning with respect for the integrity of life and the planet on which it has evolved. This is the future of life science education.

Summary
of
Recommendations

1. Biology teachers should emphasize active, inquiry-based learning and engage their students in the doing of science.

2. Hands-on exercises should be pursued, but not at the expense of animal lives; countless ways exist for achieving exciting, engaging hands-on exercises for students (e.g., having students study themselves, and outdoor studies of animals and plants).

3. The time required to perform good-quality dissections should be used instead to make room for more pressing life science topics such as cell biology, molecular genetics, evolution, biochemistry, environmental science, and animal behavior.

4. Teacher training should be reformed so that exposure to alternatives is included and dissection of animals is not a training prerequisite for obtaining a science teaching license.

5. Students should be fully involved in ethical decision making in the classroom.

6. Conscientious objection should not be seen as rebelliousness aimed at disrupting a teacher's efforts to teach, but rather, respected as evidence of concern and reflection.

7. Concern for animals should not be labeled as "squeamishness" but should be acknowledged as a legitimate manifestation of empathy for others. "Squeamish" students ought not be pressured or humiliated into participation in exercises they find distasteful.

8. Teachers and students should be made more aware of the connection between cruelty to animals and interpersonal violence; though mutilation of dissected specimens may only reflect a temporary desensitization, it should not be ignored as a possible sign that a student is prone to antisocial behavior.

9. Ethics should be part of the education of all children, and dissections should not be conducted in the absence of ethical discussion about the origins of the animals and the moral implications of using them.

10. Animal dissection should be eliminated from the precollege curriculum.

11. All procurement of animals for dissection should be from ethical sources, such as animal shelters, veterinary clinics, and wildlife rehabilitation facilities. Guardian-consent programs should be established so that cats (and other companion animals) who have died or been euthanized for medical or humane reasons can be donated from shelters or veterinary clinics to schools for educational use. These cadavers should replace the supply of cats from random sources, fetal pigs from slaughterhouses, frogs from wetlands, etc.

12. The United States Department of Agriculture (USDA), which is responsible for inspecting biological supply companies (classified by the USDA as "Class B Dealers"), should begin requiring biological supply companies to provide annual reports. These reports should include the numbers and species of animals killed and sold to schools for educational use, and the methods of capturing, transporting, handling, and killing the animals.

13. Biological supply companies should be required to conduct environmental impact assessments prior to collecting from wild animal populations.

14. Students should be informed of the specifics regarding the sources of animals used in the classroom, including methods used for capturing, transporting, handling, and killing the animals.

15. Dissection of species whose populations are known to be overexploited and/or in decline (e.g., leopard frogs, bullfrogs, spiny dogfish sharks) should be discontinued.

16. Students involved in dissections should be provided with gloves, masks, and safety instruction to minimize the hazards of exposure to formaldehyde.

17. Science teacher training should, without exception, include training in the use of computer simulations and other alternatives resources, including alternatives databases and loan programs.

18. School exercises that involve killing, undernourishing, or otherwise harming live animals should be replaced with humane alternatives, such as computer simulations, observational and behavioral field study, and benign investigations of the students themselves.

19. The traditional frog- and turtle-pithing exercises should be terminated and replaced with computer packages, which have been shown to save time and money without compromising educational value. Studies that involve the students as investigators and subjects should be more widely adopted.

20. Medical schools still using live terminal dog labs should follow the lead of other schools that have replaced these procedures with humane alternatives.

21. Veterinary schools should accelerate the current trend towards replacement of purpose-bred and/or healthy animals with clinical cases for surgical training, including spay/neuter of shelter animals.

22. Recognizing that perioperative experience, including handling live tissue, is a critical part of a veterinary education, student participation in actual clinical cases coupled with primary surgical experience performing procedures of benefit to the animal (e.g., spay/neuter of shelter animals) should wholly replace traditional "survival" surgeries.

23. For common surgeries that are not medically required by an individual animal, only two options should exist: (1) terminal surgery on anesthetized terminally ill animals with guardian consent, or (2) cadaver surgery where cadavers are ethically obtained.

24. All science fairs should abide by a policy against inflicting deliberate harm on sentient animals.

25. Laws should be implemented that require a certain level of competency before a person is allowed to conduct animal experiments.

26. All students should have a legally mandated right to use humane alternatives to dissection and other classroom exercises harmful to animals. Currently, fewer than one in five American states have statewide laws or policies mandating student choice in dissection. The result is that some students are granted rights denied to others. States still lacking such laws should make their enactment a high priority.

27. Dissection choice laws should apply to students at all levels of education; currently, such laws apply only to precollege students and exclude post-secondary students even though the validity of conscientious objection is independent of learning level.

28. IACUCs should apply more stringent restrictions on proposals for animal use in instruction and should always look for ways to piggyback teaching exercises that involve animals into ongoing research at the institution.

Literature Cited

Abdi, S.N.M. 1998. Non-violence group wins dissection ban. *South China Morning Post*, 29 May.

Adkins, J., and R. Lock. 1994. Using animals in secondary education: A pilot survey. *Journal of Biological Education* 28(1): 48-52.

Alternatives in education: New approaches for a new millennium. 1999. 33 min. EuroNICHE. Videotape.

American Medical Student Association. 1993. Preamble, purposes and principles. Reston, Va.: American Medical Student Association.

American School Board Journal. 1992. Ballot box: Finding—Don't eliminate dissection (January): 56.

American Veterinary Medical Association (AVMA). 1993. Report of the AVMA Panel on Euthanasia. *Journal of the American Veterinary Medical Association* 202(2): 229-49.

———. 1998. *Accreditation Policies and Procedures of the Committee on Veterinary Technician Education and Activities (CVTEA).* Schaumburg, Ill.: AVMA.

Ammons, S.W. 1995. Use of live animals in the curricula of U.S. medical schools in 1994. *Academic Medicine* 70:740-43.

Animal Welfare Act (AWA) Docket No. 91-75. 1994. *United States Department of Agriculture vs. Carolina Biological Supply Company.* March 30.

Animal Welfare Act (AWA) Docket No. 93-118. 1993. *[USDA Class B dealer Al Wise barred from dealing in cats]* July 7.

Arluke, A., and F. Hafferty. 1996. From apprehension to fascination with dog lab: The use of absolutions by medical students. *Journal of Contemporary Ethnography* 25(2): 201-25.

Asada, Y., M. Tsuzuki, S. Akiyama, N.Y. Macer, and D.R.J. Macer. 1996. High school teaching of bioethics in New Zealand, Australia, and Japan. *Journal of Moral Education* 25(4): 401-20.

Associated Press. 1995. 800 cats killed for U.S. research found in piles on Mexican ranch. *Houston Chronicle*, 8 April.

AVMA. *See* American Veterinary Medical Association.

Awwad, A.M. 1984. A training card for microsurgery. *Microsurgery* 5:160.

Balcombe, J.P. 1994. Letter to the editor: More on animal rights. *The American Biology Teacher* 56(6): 330.

———. 1996. Dissection and the law. *The AV Magazine* 105(3): 18-21.

———. 1997a. Student/teacher conflict regarding animal dissection. *The American Biology Teacher* 59(1): 22-25.

———. 1997b. Animals in education: Overcoming barriers to acceptance. In *Animal Alternatives, Welfare and Ethics*, edited by L.F.M. van Zutphen and M. Balls. New York: Elsevier.

———. 1998. Letter to the editor. *The American Biology Teacher* 60(8): 565-66.

———. 1999. Courses on animals and society: A growing trend in post-secondary education. *Animals and Society* 7(3):229-40.

———. In press. *Animal Use in Education: Global Overview of Current Law and Policy.* Amsterdam: Elsevier.

Barnard, N.D., and L. Baron. 1989. Alternatives to dissection. *Humane Innovations and Alternatives in Animal Experimentation* 3:92-93.

Barnard, N.D., J. Stolz, and L. Baron. 1988. Use of and alternatives to animals in laboratory courses at U.S. medical schools. *Journal of Medical Education* 63(September): 720-22.

Barr, G.E., and H.A. Herzog. In press. The high school dissection experience. *Society and Animals.*

Bauer, M.S. 1993. A survey of the use of live animals, cadavers, inanimate models, and computers in teaching veterinary surgery. *Journal of the American Veterinary Medical Association* 203(7): 1047-51.

Bauer, M.S., and H.B. Seim III. 1992. Alternative methods to teach veterinary surgery. *Humane Innovations and Alternatives* 6:401-4.

Bauer, M.S., N. Glickman, S.K. Salisbury, J.P. Toombs, and J.M. Prostredny. 1992a. Surgical vs. terminal animal laboratories to teach small animal surgery. *Journal of Veterinary Medical Education* 19(2): 54-58.

Bauer, M.S., N. Glickman, L. Glickman, J.P. Toombs, and P. Bill. 1992b. Evaluation of the effectiveness of a cadaver laboratory during a fourth-year veterinary surgery rotation. *Journal of Veterinary Medical Education* 19(3): 77-84.

Bauhardt, V. 1990. Veranderung der einstellung gegenuber gliedertieren durch interaktion mit lebenden tieren im biologieunterricht, Diss. In *Munchner schriften zur didaktik der biologie,* edited by W. Killermann. Munich: University of Munich.

Bealer, J. 1980. Classroom study of the diet of a barn owl. *The American Biology Teacher* 42(6): 342-44.

Beardsley, T. 1992. Teaching real science. *Scientific American* (October): 98-108.

Bekoff, M. 1999. Dissection: An unkind cut? *Sunday Camera,* 14 March, 12F.

Bennett, J. 1994. New survey shows Colorado students want a choice. *Good Medicine* 3(3): 6.

Bentley, B. 1991. Animal use in the classroom [review of Hairston, R.V., 1990, *The responsible use of animals in biology classrooms—including alternatives to dissection,* NABT, Reston, Va]. *The Quarterly Review of Biology* 66: 475-77.

Berman, W. 1984. Dissection dissected. *The Science Teacher* 51(6): 42-49.

Beyers, D. 1996. On-line algebra students are in a class by themselves. *Washington Post,* 19 February, A1.

Blaustein, A.R., and D.B. Wake. 1995. The puzzle of declining amphibian populations. *Scientific American* (April): 52-57.

Blumenstyk, G. 1996. Government fines and citations force colleges to address on-the-job dangers. *The Chronicle of Higher Education* 42.

Bonner, B.B., D. Eng, and O. Feingold. 1989. Bacteriology in wild and warehoused red-eared slider turtles, *Trachemys scripta elegans.* In Proceedings of the Thirteenth Annual International Herpetological Symposium on Captive Propagation and Husbandry, 1-9. Phoenix, Ariz., June.

Bosco, J. 1986. An analysis of evaluations of interactive video. *Educational Technology* (May): 7-17.

Bowd, A.D. 1993. Dissection as an instructional technique in secondary science: Choice and alternatives. *Society and Animals* 1(1): 83-88.

Brennan, A. 1997. Animals in teaching: Education and ethics. In *Animals in education: Value, responsibilities and questions,* edited by A. Brennan and R. Einstein. Glen Osmond, South Australia: ANZCCART.

Broida, J., L. Tingley, R. Kimball, and J. Miele. 1993. Personality differences between pro- and anti-vivisectionists. *Society and Animals* 1(2): 129-45.

Brown, G., G. Collins, D. Dewhurst, and I. Hughes. 1998. Computer simulations in teaching neuromuscular physiology—time for a change from traditional methods? *Alternatives to Laboratory Animals* 16: 163-74.

Brown, L.M. 1989. A demographic comparison of the perceptions of ninth grade students toward dissection and other uses of animals. Teacher Leader Program thesis, College of Education and Human Services, Wright State University, Dayton, Ohio.

Brown, M.J., P.T. Pearson, and F.N. Thompson. 1993. Guidelines for animal surgery in research and teaching. *Journal of the American Veterinary Medical Association* 54(9): 1544-59.

Buettinger, C. 1997. Women and antivivisection in late nineteenth-century America. *Journal of Social History* 30(4): 857-72.

Burns, J.P., F.E. Reardon, and R.D. Truog. 1994. Using newly deceased patients to teach resuscitation procedures. *New England Journal of Medicine* 331(24): 1652-55.

Bushby, P.A. 1997. Spotlight on a school: Mississippi State University. *Alternatives in Veterinary Medical Education* 6:4-5.

Buyukmihci, N.C. 1995. Non-violence in surgical training. Association of Veterinarians for Animal Rights (AVAR) unpublished document.

Canadian Council on Animal Care (CCAC). 1999. CCAC survey of animal use 1996. *Resource* 22(2): 1-16.

Carley, W. 1998. Letters: Like and unlike—An open letter to Alicia Silverstone and People for the Ethical Treatment of Animals. *The American Biology Teacher* 60(6): 406.

Carlson, P. 1995. *Alternatives in medical education: Nonanimal methods.* Washington, D.C.: Physicians Committee for Responsible Medicine.

Carolina Biological Supply Company (CBSC). 1994. Letter and press release to The HSUS from CBSC President Peter Tourtellot, 26 May.

Carpenter, K. 1992. Animal dissection promotes hot debate at Darien High School. *Darien (Conn.) News-Review,* 4 June, A1: 13, 28.

Carpenter, L.G., D.L. Piermattei, M.D. Salman, E.C. Orton, A.W. Nelson, D.D. Smeak, P.B. Jennings, and R.A. Taylor. 1991. A comparison of surgical training with live anesthetized dogs and cadavers. *Veterinary Surgery* 20: 373-78.

Cavalieri, P., and P. Singer. 1993. *The great ape project: Equality beyond humanity.* London: Fourth Estate.

CBSC. *See* Carolina Biological Supply Company.

CCAC. *See* Canadian Council on Animal Care.

Clarke, K. 1987. The use of microcomputer simulations in undergraduate neurophysiology experiments. *Alternatives to Laboratory Animals* 14: 134-40.

Clifton, M. 1992. Dissection: A cutting edge debate. *Animal People* (August).

Cochrane, W., and A. Dockerty. 1984. The role of dissection in schools. *Biologist* 31(5): 250-54.

Cohen, P.S., and Block, M. 1991. Replacement of laboratory animals in an introductory psychology laboratory. *Humane Innovations and Alternatives* 5: 221-25.

Cole, K.C. 1990. Science under scrutiny. *New York Times,* 7 January.

Coppa, G.F., and M.S. Nachbar. 1997. Virtual reality: An alternative to animal use? In *Animal alternatives, welfare and ethics,* edited by L.F.M. van Zutphen and M. Balls. Amsterdam: Elsevier.

Critical Concepts, Inc.(CCI). 1999. Critical Concepts releases physiology simulation on CD-ROM: Academia can save thousands using computer simulations. Company press release, 15 April, *www.laketech.com.*

Dairy and Nutrition Council. 1987. *The Great Grow Along! A tail of two rats and you!* Indianapolis, Ind.: Dairy and Nutrition Council.

Dalby, D.H. 1970. Plant taxonomy as a field study. *Journal of Biological Education* 4(2). In *Ecology projects: Ideas and practicals from the Journal of Biological Education,* edited by D. Harding. Institute of Biology, London, Queensbury Place.

de Greeve, P. 1989. Education and training of animal technicians in the Netherlands. In *Animal experimentation: legislation and education,* edited by L.R.M. van Zutphen, H. Rozemond, and A.C. Beynen. Veterinary Public Health Inspectorate, Rijswijk.

Utrecht, Netherlands: Department of Laboratory Animal Science.

Dennis, M.B. 1999. Alternative training methods II: Incorporating inanimate surgical models. *Lab Animal* 28(5): 32-36.

DeRosa, B., ed. 1998. *For the birds!: Activities to replace chick hatching in the K-6 classroom.* East Haddam, Conn.: National Association for Humane and Environmental Education (NAHEE).

Dewhurst, D.G., and L. Jenkinson. 1995. The impact of computer-based alternatives on the use of animals in undergraduate teaching. *Alternatives to Laboratory Animals* 23: 521-30.

Dewhurst, D.G., and A.S. Meehan. 1993. Evaluation of the use of computer simulations of experiments in teaching undergraduate students. *British Journal of Pharmacology Proceedings Supplement* 108: 238.

Dewhurst, D.G., J. Hardcastle, P.T. Hardcastle, and E. Stuart. 1994. Comparison of a computer simulation program and a traditional laboratory practical class for teaching the principles of intestinal absorption. *American Journal of Physiology* 267 (Advances in Physiology Education 12/1): S95-S104.

DeYoung, D.J., and D.C. Richardson. 1987. Teaching the principles of internal fixation of fractures with plastic bone models. *Journal of Veterinary Medical Education* 14: 30-31.

Downie, J.R. 1989. Uses of animals in teaching biology: Attitudes of staff and students towards the teaching of bio-ethics. In *Animal Use in Education,* edited by B.S. Close, F. Dolins, and G. Mason. London: Humane Education Centre.

Downie, R. 1993. The teaching of bioethics in the higher education of biologists. *Journal of Biological Education* 27(1): 34-38.

Downie, R., and J. Meadows. 1995. Experience with a dissection opt-out scheme in university level biology. *Journal of Biological Education* 29(3): 187-94.

Dudlicek, J. 1998. Schools offer alternatives to dissection of animals. *Calumet City (Ill.)Star,* 5 April.

Duffy, N. 1999. Alternative training methods I: Proceedings of the 1998 LAWTE meeting. *Lab Animal* 28(5): 24-28.

Duncan, H. 1999. Dissection moves into digital age. *Elmira (N.Y.) Star-Gazette,* 5 November.

Eisnitz, G. 1997. *Slaughterhouse: The shocking story of greed, neglect, and inhumane treatment inside the U.S. meat industry.* Amherst, N.Y.: Prometheus.

Emmons, M.B. 1980. Secondary and elementary school use of live and preserved animals. In *Animals in Education: Use of animals in high school biology classes and science fairs,* edited by H. McGiffin and N. Brownley. Washington, D.C.: The Institute for the Study of Animal Problems.

Erickson, H.H., and V.L. Clegg. 1993. Active learning in cardiovascular physiology. In *Promoting active learning in the life science classroom,* edited by H.I. Modell and J.A. Michael. Annals of the New York Academy of Sciences, vol. 701. New York: New York Academy of Sciences.

Fawver, A.L., C.E. Branch, L. Trentham, B.T. Robertson, and S.D. Beckett. 1990. A comparison of interactive videodisc instruction with live animal laboratories. *American Journal of Physiology* 259 (Advances in Physiology Education 4): S11-S14.

Finch, P.A. 1988. Why this is not a lab report. *Children and Animals* (April/May): 2.

Fingland, R. 1999. After alternatives. *Alternatives in Veterinary Medical Education* 10: 1, 6.

Fleming, D. 1952. *Science and technology in Providence 1760-1914: An essay in the history of Brown University in the metropolitan community.* Providence, R.I.: Brown University.

Foreman, J. 1992. Physicians support use of animals in medical education. *Archives of Ophthalmology* 110: 324.

Fowler, H.S., and E.J. Brosius. 1968. A research study on the values gained from dissection of animals in secondary school biology. *Science Education* 52(2): 55-57.

Francione, G.L., and A. E. Charlton. 1992. *Vivisection and dissection in the classroom: A guide to conscientious objection.* Jenkintown, Pa.: American Anti–Vivisection Society.

Freeman, S. 1995. Students choose cats over computer models. *Union News/Sunday Republican* (Springfield, Mass.), 10 December.

Gammage, P. 1982. *Children and Schooling: Issues in Childhood Socialization.* Reading, Mass.: Allen and Unwin.

Gibbs, W.W., and D. Fox. 1999. The false crisis in science education. *Scientific American* 281(4): 87-93.

Gibbs, E.L., T.J. Gibbs, and P.C. VanDyck. 1966. *Rana pipiens*: Health and disease. *Laboratory Animal Care* 16(2): 142-60.

Gibbs, E.L., G.W. Nace, and M.B. Emmons. 1971. The live frog is almost dead. *BioScience* 21: 1027-34.

Gilmore, D.R. 1991a. Politics and prejudice: Dissection in biology education, part I. *The American Biology Teacher* 53(4): 211-13.

———. 1991b. Politics and prejudice: Dissection in biology education, part II. *The American Biology Teacher* 53(5): 272-74.

Goldfinger, J. 1993. Dissecting need for animal tests in biology lab. *Courier Times* (Levittown-Bristol, Pa.), 16 December.

Goleman, D. 1997. *Emotional intelligence.* New York: Bantam Books.

Greenfield, C.L., A.L. Johnson, M.W. Arends, and A.J. Wroblewski. 1993. Development of parenchymal abdominal organ models for use in teaching veterinary soft tissue surgery. *Veterinary Surgery* 22(5): 357-62.

Greenfield, C.L., A.L. Johnson, D.J. Shaeffer, and L.L. Hungerford. 1995. Comparison of surgical skills of veterinary students trained using models or live animals. *Journal of the American Veterinary Medical Association* 206(12): 1840-45.

Greenwald, G.S. 1985. ACDP survey on use of animals in teaching physiology. *Physiologist* 28: 478-80.

Griffith, S. 1991. Severing students from a tradition. *The Washington Post,* 17 December, D1, D4.

Guy, J.F., and A.J. Frisby. 1992. Using interactive videodiscs to teach gross anatomy to undergraduates at The Ohio State University. *Academic Medicine* 67: 132-33.

Hairston, R.V., ed. 1990. *The responsible use of animals in biology classrooms: Including alternatives to dissection.* Monograph 4. Reston, Va.: NABT.

Hale, P. 1989. Eye surgeons can now practice skills on mannequin. *Star-Observer* (Hudson, Wis.), 20 April, 1B, 3C.

Hamm, T.E., and J.R. Blum. 1992. The humane use of animals in teaching. *American Association for Laboratory Animal Science* 31(5): 20-25.

Hancock, E. 1995. The boy who died too fast. *Johns Hopkins Magazine,* 25 February.

Hancock, J.M. 1991. *Biology is outdoors! A comprehensive resource for studying school environments.* Portland, Maine: J. Weston Walch.

Harding, D. 1992. *Ecology projects: Ideas and practicals from the Journal of Biological Education.* London: The Institute of Biology.

Heim, A. 1981. The desensitization of teacher and students. In *Humane education– A symposium,* edited by D. Paterson. Burgess Hill, England. Humane Education Council.

Heiman, M. 1987. Learning to learn: A behavioral approach to improving thinking. In *Thinking: The Second International Conference,* edited by D.N.Perkins, J. Lochhead, and J. Bishop. Hillsdale, N.J.: Lawrence Erlbaum Associates.

Heintzelman, D.S. 1983. *The birdwatcher's activity book.* Harrisburg, Pa.: Stackpole Books.

Hendricks, G., and K. Hendricks. 1992. *Conscious loving: The journey to co-commitment.* New York: Bantam Books.

Henman, M.C., and G.D.H. Leach. 1983. An alternative method for pharmacology laboratory class instruction using biovideograph video tape recordings. *British Journal of Pharmacology* 80: 591P.

Hepner, L.H. 1994. *Animals in education: The facts, issues and implications.* Albuquerque: Richmond Publishers.

Hertzfeldt, R. 1994. Area high school students find approval in the dissection law. *The Sun* (York, Pa.), 30 April.

Hine, R.L., B.L. Les, and B.F. Hellmich. 1981. Leopard frog populations and mortality in Wisconsin, 1974-76. *Technical Bulletin No. 122,* Wisconsin Department of Natural Resources, 1-39.

Holden, C. 1990. Animal rights activism threatens dissection. *Science,* Vol, 250, 9 November, 751.

Holmberg, D.L., and J.R. Cockshutt. 1994. A nonanimal alternative for teaching introductory surgery. *Humane Innovations and Alternatives* 8: 635-37.

Holmberg, D.L., J.R. Cockshutt, and A.W.P. Basher. 1993. Use of a dog abdominal surrogate for teaching surgery. *Journal of Veterinary Medical Education* 20(2): 61-62.

Howard, W.E. 1990. *Animal rights versus nature.* Davis, Calif.: W.E. Howard.

———. 1993. Letters: Animal research is defensible. *Journal of Mammalogy* 74(1): 234-35.

Huang, S.D., and J. Aloi. 1991. The impact of using interactive video in teaching general biology. *The American Biology Teacher* 53(5): 281-84.

Humane Society of the United States (HSUS). 1993. Guidelines for the study of animals in elementary and secondary school biology. Washington, D.C.: HSUS.

———. 1994. General statement regarding euthanasia methods for dogs and cats. Washington, D.C.: HSUS.

———. 1996. *The dissection controversy: Bridging the teacher-student gap.* Three-part videotape of a one-day symposium held at the National Association of Biology Teachers convention, 16 September, Charlotte, North Carolina.

HSUS. *See* Humane Society of the United States.

Iacono, G, F. Cavataio, G. Montalto et al. 1998. Intolerance of cow's milk and chronic constipation in children. *New England Journal of Medicine* 339: 1100-14.

Intelitool. 1998. Physiogrip and Spriocomp: Capabilities and features. Promotional brochures, *www.com/intelitool/.*

Jacobs, D., and R. Moore. 1998. Concept-driven teaching and assessment in invertebrate zoology. *Journal of Biological Education* 32(3): 191-99.

Jayaraman, K.S. 1987. India bans frog trade. *Animal Welfare Institute Quarterly* (Spring/Summer).

Johnson, A.L., and J.A. Farmer. 1989. Evaluation of traditional and alternative models in psychomotor laboratories for veterinary surgery. *Journal of Veterinary Medical Education* 16(1): 11-14.

Johnson, A.L., J. Harari, J. Lincoln, J.A. Farmer, and D. Korvick. 1990. Bone models of pathologic conditions used for teaching veterinary orthopedic surgery. *Journal of Veterinary Medical Education* 17: 13-15.

Johnson, S. n.d. *The ethical scientist: Alternatives in education and research.* Tonbridge, England: Animal Aid.

Jones, N.A., R.P. Olafson, and J. Sutin. 1978. Evaluation of a gross anatomy program without dissection. *Journal of Medical Education* 53: 198-205.

Jones, R.L., and C. Borchert. 1999. Spotlight on a school: Colorado State University. *Alternatives in Veterinary Medical Education* 11: 4-5.

Jordan, W. 1991. Reason, humanity, and the uses of animals in the classroom. *Wigwag* (February): 23-31.

Karjalainen, J., J.M. Martin, M. Knip, J. Ilonen, B.H. Robinson, E. Savilahti, H.K. Akerblom, and H.M. Dosch. 1992. A bovine albumin peptide as a possible trigger of insulin-dependent diabetes mellitus. *New England Journal of Medicine* 327: 302-7.

Kaufman, T., D.J. Hurwitz, and D.L. Ballantyne. 1984. The foliage leaf in microvascular surgery. *Microsurgery* 5: 57-58.

Keiser, T.D., and R.W. Hamm. 1991. Forum: Dissection—The case for. *The Science Teacher* 58(1): 13-15.

Keith-Spiegel, P.C., B.G. Tabachnick, and M. Allen. 1993. Ethics and academia: Students' views of professors' actions. *Ethics and Behavior* 3(2): 149-62.

Kellert, S.R. 1985. Attitudes toward animals: Age-related development among children. *Journal of Environmental Education* 16(3): 29-39.

———. 1989. Perceptions of animals in America. In *Perceptions of animals in American culture,* edited by R.J. Hoage. Washington, D.C.: Smithsonian Institution Press.

———. 1996. *The value of life: Biological diversity and human society.* Washington, D.C.: Island Press.

Kelly, D. 1991. Use of animals in medical education. Report from the conference, Animal Care and Use Programs: Regulatory Compliance and Education in an Age of Fiscal Constraint, Boston, Massachusetts, 21-22 March.

Kelly, J.A. 1986. Alternatives to aversive procedures with animals in the psychology teaching setting. In *Advances in Animal Welfare Science,* 1985/86, edited by M.W. Fox and L.D. Mickley. Washington, D.C.: HSUS.

Kennedy, D. 1997. *Academic duty.* Cambridge, Mass.: Harvard University Press.

Keown, D.H. 1994. Demonstrating variation within the species. In *Investigating evolutionary biology in the laboratory,* edited by W.F. McComas. Lancaster, Pa.: Lancaster Press.

Kerstetter, J. 1993. Free the frogs: Ashland policy allows students to skip science dissections. *Ashland News* (Boston), June.

Killermann, W. 1998. Research into biology teaching methods. *Journal of Biological Education* 33(1): 4-9.

King, E. 1994. Ready, set, slice: If it's spring, it must be time to dissect those frogs. *Washington Post,* 7 April.

Kingsmill, S. 1990. Bullfrog blues: Where have all the bullfrogs gone? *Seasons* 30(2): 16-19, 36.

Kinzie, M.B., R. Strauss, and J. Foss. 1993. The effects of an interactive dissection simulation on the performance and achievement of high school biology students. *Journal of Research in Science Teaching* 30(8): 989-1000.

Klassan, M. 1991. Losing their spots: No one knows why leopard frogs are disappearing from Alberta. *Nature Canada* 20(1): 9-11.

Knight, A. 1998. Refusing to quit: How we won the right to conscientiously object at Murdoch University. *Animals Today* (August-October): 18-20.

———. 1999. Alternatives to harmful animal usage in tertiary education. *ANZCCART News* 12(1): 10-11.

Krause, L.M. 1980. Student (and animal) welfare. In *Animals in education: Use of animals in high school biology classes and science fairs,* edited by H. McGiffin and N. Brownley. Washington, D.C.: The Institute for the Study of Animal Problems.

Krause, R.A. 1994. Cutting edge: Schools offer dissection options. *Post-Tribune* (Gary, Ind.), 14 November.

Krutch, J.W. 1956. *The Great Chain of Life.* New York: Pyramid Books.

Kuhn, D.J. 1990. Reading aloud and the heart rate. *The American Biology Teacher* 52(3): 168-70.

Kulik, J.A., C.L. Kulik, and P.A. Cohen. 1980. Effectiveness of computer-based college teaching: A meta-analysis. *Review of Education Research* 50: 525-44.

Langley, G. 1989. A plea for sensitive science. In *Animal experimentation: The consensus changes,* edited by G. Langley. Houndsmills, England: Macmillan Press.

Larson, S. 1998. *Beyond dissection: Innovative teaching tools for biology education.* Boston, Mass.: Ethical Science Education Coalition.

Lavine, R. 1993. Problem solving in neurobiology using clinical case studies in small groups. In *Promoting active learning in the life science classroom,* edited by H.I. Modell and J.A. Michael. Annals of the New York Academy of Sciences, vol. 701. New York.

Leathard, H.L., and D.G. Dewhurst. 1995. Comparison of the cost-effectiveness of a computer-assisted learning program with a tutored demonstration to teach intestinal motility to medical students. *Association for Learning Technology Journal* 3(1): 118-25.

Leavitt, E.S. and B. Beary. 1990. Humane education in the public schools. In *Animals and their legal rights: A survey of American laws from 1641 to 1990.* Washington, D.C.: Animal Welfare Institute.

Le Duc, T. 1946. *Piety and intellect at Amherst College 1865-1912.* New York: Columbia University Press.

Legislative Research Inc. n.d. *Legislative History of Education Code Sections 32255.1, 32255.3, 32255.4, 32255.5, 32255.6 as added by Statutes of 1988, Chapter 65, Section 1, Assembly Bill 2507—Speier, relating to education.* Sacramento, Calif.: Legislative Research Inc.

Leonard, W.H. 1992. A comparison of student performance following instruction by interactive videodisc versus conventional laboratory. *Journal of Research in Science Teaching* 29(1): 93-102.

Lewis, R. 1999. Fetal pig shortage hamstrings biology instructors. *The Scientist* 13(3): 8.

Lieb, M.J. 1985. Dissection: A valuable motivational tool or a trauma to the high school student? Master's thesis, National College of Education, Evanston, Illinois.

Lien, J. 1993. Student attitudes and how they are influenced. In Proceedings from Biology Education and Animals: Opportunities and Issues, a Tufts University School of Veterinary Medicine, Center for Animals and Public Policy workshop, Washington, D.C., 22 April.

Lilienfield, L.S., and N.C. Broering. 1994. Computers as teachers: learning from animations. *American Journal of Physiology* 11(1): Advances in Physiology Education, S47-S54.

Lluka, L., and B. Oelrichs. 1999. Replacement and reduction of animal usage in teaching physiology and pharmacology at the University of Queensland. *ANZCCART News* 12(2): 4-7.

Lock, R. 1994. Dissection as an instructional technique in secondary science: Comment on Bowd. *Society and Animals* 2(1): 67-73.

Lock, R., and K. Millett. 1991. The Animals and Science Education Project, 1990-1991. University of Birmingham School of Education.

Lockwood, R. 1989. Following your conscience in the classroom: An interview with Jenifer Graham. *HSUS News* (Winter): 27-29.

Lockwood, R., and F. Ascione. 1998. *Cruelty to animals and interpersonal violence.* West Lafayette, Ind.: Purdue University Press.

Loiacono, R. 1998. Animal replacement and reduction: Multimedia teaching aids in behavioural pharmacology. *ANZCCART News* 11(2): 4-5.

Long, D. 1997. Cutting to the conscience. *The Tennesseean* (Nashville), 13 October.

Lord, T.R. 1990. The importance of animal dissection. *Journal of College Science Teaching* (May): 330-31.

Lord, T.R., and R. Moses. 1994. College students' opinions about animal dissections. *Journal of College Science Teaching* 23(5): 267-70.

Marbury, S. 1994. Hog industry insider. *Feedstuffs*, 2 May, 58-59.

Marquardt, K. 1993. Animal rightists using schools to further cause. *Farm Talk* (Parsons, Kans.), 17 February.

Mason, J., and P. Singer. 1990. *Animal factories*. New York: Harmony Books.

Martinsville Reporter (Indianapolis). 1996. Morgan County Humane Society sad, angry over puppy's death, dissection, 19 September.

Matthews, D. 1998a. Comparison of *MacPig* to fetal pig dissection in college biology. *The American Biology Teacher* 60(3): 228-29.

———. 1998b. Efficacy of fetal pig dissection alternatives questioned. *The American Biology Teacher* 61(2): 88.

Mayer, V.J., and N.K. Hinton. 1990. Animals in the classroom: Considering the options. *The Science Teacher* 57(3): 27-30.

Mayer, W.V. 1982. *Guidelines for educational priorities and curricular innovations on issues in human/animal interactions*. Boulder, Colo.: Biological Sciences Curriculum Study.

Mayr, E. 1982. *The growth of biological thought*. Cambridge, Mass.: Belknap Press.

McCaffrey, S. 1995. Computerized mannequins: A new era in medical training. *Good Medicine* (Autumn): 8-9.

McCollum, T.L. 1987. The effect of animal dissections on student acquisition of knowledge of and attitudes toward the animals dissected. Ph.D. diss., University of Cincinnati.

McGregor, J.C. 1980. The use of the placenta for microsurgical vascular practice. *Royal College of Surgeons at Edinburgh Journal* 25: 233-36.

McInerney, J. 1993. Animals in education: Are we prisoners of false sentiment? *The American Biology Teacher* 55(5): 276-80.

McKenna, C. 1998. *Fashion victims: An inquiry into the welfare of animals on fur farms*. London: World Society for the Protection of Animals.

McKernan, R.A. 1991. Student opinions about the use of dissection in science classes. Planning, Research and Accountability report. Albuquerque Public Schools.

McNaught, S. 1998. Learning not to kill. *Boston Phoenix*, 26 February-5 March.

Medvedev, Z.A. 1971. *The rise and fall of T.D. Lysenko*. New York.: Columbia University Press.

Michael, J. A. 1993. Teaching problem solving in small groups. In *Promoting active learning in the life science classroom*, edited by H.I. Modell and J.A. Michael. Annals of the New York Academy of Sciences, vol. 701. New York.

Milgram, S. 1974. *Obedience to authority*. New York: Harper and Row.

Millett, K., and R. Lock. 1992. GCSE students' attitudes towards animal use: Some implications for biology/science teachers. *Journal of Biological Education* 26(3): 204-8.

Modell, H.I., and J.A. Michael, eds. *Promoting active learning in the life science classroom*. Annals of the New York Academy of Sciences, vol. 701. New York.

More, D., and C.L. Ralph. 1992. A test of effectiveness of courseware in a college biology class. *Journal of Educational Technology Systems* 21: 79-84.

Moredun. n.d. *Interactive veterinary simulators* (product brochure). Penicuik, Scotland.

Morley, D. 1978. *The sensitive scientist: Report of a British association study group*, 84-91. London: SCM.

Morrison, A.R. 1992. Letters to the editor. *The American Biology Teacher* 54(3): 135-36.

Morton, D.B. 1987. Animal use in education and the alternatives. *Alternatives to Laboratory Animals* 14: 334-43.

Nab, J. 1989. Alternatives in education. In *Animal experimentation: Legislation and education*, edited by L.R.M. van Zutphen, H. Rozemond, and A.C. Beynen. Veterinary Public Health Inspectorate, Rijswijk. Utrecht, Netherlands: Department of Laboratory Animal Science.

NABT. *See* National Association of Biology Teachers.

National Association of Biology Teachers (NABT). 1981. *The use of animals in biology education*. Reston, Va.: NABT.

———. 1995. *The use of animals in biology education*. Reston, Va.: NABT.

———. 1999. Letter from Lisa Walter, convention director, to the National Anti-Vivisection Society, 15 June. Reston, Va.: NABT

National Research Council (NRC). 1990. *Fulfilling the promise: Biology education in the nation's schools*. Washington, D.C.: National Academy Press.

National Student Nurses Association (NSNA). 1997. NSNA policies: Cat dissection. *NSNA handbook: Getting the pieces to fit*. New York: NSNA.

Nebraska Scientific. n.d. Everything you wanted to know about fetal pigs, but didn't know who to ask (brochure). Omaha, Nebr.

Newsome, J., M. Piekarczyk, and L. Rutter. 1993. Alternatives to live animal models in laser surgery training. *AWIC Newsletter* 4(3): 3-4.

Nolte, B. 1999. Graham vo-ag teacher charged in pig's death. *Urbana Daily Citizen*, 19 May, A1, A5.

Nosek, T.M., G.C. Bond, J.M. Ginsburg, R.E. Godt, W.F. Hofman, W.J. Jackson, T.F. Ogle, S.P. Porterfield, S.D. Stoney, Jr., V.T. Wiedmeier, J.A. Work, L.A. Lewis, and M. Levy. 1993. Using computer-aided instruction (CAI) to promote active learning in the physiology classroom. In *Promoting active learning in the life science classroom*, edited by H.I. Modell and J.A. Michael. Annals of the New York Academy of Sciences, vol. 701. New York.

NRC. *See* National Research Council.

Office of Technology Assessment (OTA). 1986. Animal use in education and the alternatives. In *Alternatives to animal use in research, testing and education*. Washington, D.C.: U.S. Congress.

Offner, S. 1995. Cut here. *The Executive Educator* 17: 40.

Ogilvie, D.M., and R.H. Stinson. 1992. *Discoveries in biology: Nondestructive investigations with living animals*. Toronto: Copp Clark Pitman Ltd.

Opinion Research Corporation. 1999. Animal dissection in high school science classes: Summary of results. Chicago: National Anti–Vivisection Society.

ORC. *See* Opinion Research Corporation.

Orlans, F.B. 1977. *Animal care from protozoa to small mammals* (see chapter 17, Experiments with students). Menlo Park, Calif.: Addison-Wesley.

———. 1988a. Guest editorial: Should students harm or destroy animal life? *The American Biology Teacher* 50(1): 6-12.

———. 1988b. Debating dissection: Pros, cons, and alternatives. *The Science Teacher* (November): 36-40.

———. 1991. Forum: Dissection—The case against. *The Science Teacher* 58(1): 12-14.

———. 1992. NABT Policy—"a breath of fresh air." *The American Biology Teacher* 54(3): 134.

————. 1993. *In the name of science: Issues in responsible animal experimentation.* New York: Oxford University Press.

————. 1995. Investigator competency and animal experiments: Guidelines for elementary and secondary education. *Lab Animal* 24(9): 29-34.

Orlans, F.B., T.L. Beauchamp, R. Dresser, D.B. Morton, and J.P. Gluck. 1998. *The humane use of animals: Case studies in ethical choice.* New York: Oxford University Press.

Occupational Safety and Health Administration (OSHA). n.d. Regulations (Standards - 29 CFR): Substance technical guidelines for formalin—1910.1048 App A, *www.osha.gov.*

OSHA. *See* Occupational Safety and Health Administration.

OTA. *See* Office of Technology Assessment.

Pancoast, M. 1991. Keep dissection in class. *Teacher Magazine* (September): 61.

Pankiewicz, P.R. 1995. Software review: The DynaPulse 200M. *The American Biology Teacher* 57(2): 121-22.

Patronek, G.J. 1998. Spotlight on a school: Tufts University. *Alternatives in Veterinary Medical Education* 8: 4-5.

Patronek, G.J., and A.N. Rowan. 1995. Editorial: Determining dog and cat numbers and population dynamics. *Anthrozoos* 8(4).

Pavletic, M.M., A. Schwartz, J. Berg, and D. Knapp. 1994. An assessment of the outcome of the alternative medical and surgical laboratory program at Tufts University. *Journal of the American Veterinary Medical Association* 205(1): 97-100.

PCRM. *See* Physicians Committee for Responsible Medicine.

Pease, B. 1998. Cornell student assembly unanimous: University dissection policy unacceptable. Cornell Students for the Ethical Treatment of Animals, press release, 26 March, Ithaca, New York.

Pendleton, E. 1993. Teens just say no to dissecting frogs. *Eagle Tribune* (Lawrence, Mass.), 28 March.

People for the Ethical Treatment of Animals (PETA). n.d. *Dying for biology: A special research and investigations case report.* Washington, D.C.: PETA.

Petersen, N. 1986. Dissection on a micro scale. *The Science Teacher* 53(8): 19-21.

Peterson, C.E. 1993. Use of prosection in teaching human anatomy. *Journal of College Science Teaching* (May).

Petto, A.J., and K.D. Russell. 1999. Humane education: The role of animal-based learning. In *Attitudes to animals: Views in animal welfare,* edited by F.L. Dolins. Cambridge: Cambridge University Press.

Phelps, J.L., J.O. Nilsestuen, and S. Hosemann 1992. Assessment of effectiveness of videodisc replacement of a live-animal physiology laboratory. Distinguished Papers Monograph, American Association for Respiratory Care.

Phillips, K. 1994. *Tracking the vanishing frog.* New York: St. Martin's Press.

Physicians Committee for Responsible Medicine (PCRM). 1998. *Medical school curricula with no live animal laboratories.* Washington, D.C.: PCRM.

Pifer, L., K. Shimuzu, and R. Pifer. 1994. Public attitudes toward animal research: Some international comparisons. *Society and Animals* 2(2): 95-113.

Pina, T. 1993. School board asked to require alternatives to dissection. *The Journal* (Providence, R.I.), 14 December.

Pope, S. 1997. The drive for the comprehensive use of alternatives. In *Animals in education: Value, responsibilities and questions,* edited by A. Brennan and R. Einstein. Glen Osmond, South Australia: ANZCCART.

PR Newswire. 1991. Landmark court decision supports veterinary student's right to not harm animals. Washington, D.C., 31 May.

Prentice, E.D., W.K. Metcalf, T.H. Quinn, J.G. Sharp, R.H. Jensen, and E.A. Holyoke. 1977. Stereoscopic anatomy: Evaluation of a new teaching system in human gross anatomy. *Journal of Medical Education* 52: 758-63.

Rago, P.J., K. Sosebee, J. Brodziak, and E.D. Anderson. 1994. Distribution and dynamics of Northwest Atlantic spiny dogfish *(Squalus acanthias)*. NOAA/NMFS/NEFSC Ref. Doc. 94-19.

Regan, T. 1983. *The case for animal rights.* Berkeley: University of California Press.

Reid, J.D.S., and J.A. Vestrup. 1986. Use of a simulation to teach central venous access. *Journal of Medical Education* 61: 196-97.

Reiss, M.J. 1993. Organisms for teaching. *Journal of Biological Education* 27(3): 155-56.

Rhodes, F.H.T. 1997. Rules of the game: Book review of D. Kennedy, 1997, *Academic Duty. Science* 278 (5): 1726.

Richardson, D. 1997. Student perceptions and learning outcomes of computer-assisted versus traditional instruction in physiology. *American Journal of Physiology* 273: S55-S58.

Richter, E., H. Kramer, W. Lierse, R. Maas, and K.H. Hohne. 1994. Visualization of neonatal anatomy and pathology with a new computerized three-dimensional model as a basis for teaching, diagnosis and therapy. *Acta Anatomica* 150(1): 75-79.

Rifkin, J. 1992. *Beyond beef: The rise and the fall of the cattle culture.* New York: Dutton.

Rivlin, M. 1996. Northeast "dog catchers" scratch for future. *National Fisherman* 76(10): 15-17, 76.

Robinson, R. 1996. One cell spawns a business empire. *Business—North Carolina* 5(3): 47.

Rollin, B.E. 1981. *Animal rights and human morality.* Buffalo, N.Y.: Prometheus.

Romano, M. 1995. CU settles suit over dog experiments. *Rocky Mountain News,* 1 September, 4A.

Rosenthal, J. 1994. Dissecting animals in Pennsylvania high schools is not compulsory course of study. *Tribune-Review* (Greensburg, Pa.), 3 September.

Rosse, C. 1995. The potential of computerized representations of anatomy in the training of health care providers. *Academic Medicine* 70(6): 499-505.

Rothschild, M. 1986. *Animals and Man: The Romanes Lectures 1984-5.* Oxford, England: Clarendon.

Roush, J.K. 1998. Spotlight on a school: Kansas State University. *Alternatives in Veterinary Medical Education* 9: 4-5.

Rowan, A.N. 1984. *Of mice, models, and men.* Albany: State University of New York.

Rowan, A.N. and J.C. Weer, eds. 1993. Proceedings from *Biology education and animals: Opportunities and issues,* a Tufts University School of Veterinary Medicine, Center for Animals and Public Policy workshop, 22 April, Washington, D.C.

Rowan, A.N., Loew, F.M., and Weer, J.C. 1995. *The animal research controversy: Protest, process, and public policy.* Center for Animals and Public Policy, Tufts University School of Veterinary Medicine, New Grafton, Massachusetts.

Royal Society/Institute of Biology Biological Education Committee. 1975. *Report of the working party on the dissection of animals in schools.* London: Institute of Biology.

RS/IOB. *See* Royal Society/Institute of Biology Biological Education Committee.

Russell, G.K. 1972. Vivisection and the true aims of education in biology. *The American Biology Teacher* 34: 254-57.

———. 1978. *Laboratory investigations in human physiology.* New York: Macmillan.

———. 1987. Biology: The study of life. *Orion Nature Quarterly* 6(1): 48-55.

———. 1996. Biology: The study of life. *AV Magazine* 105(3): 2-7.

Sampson, B.C. 1998. Technology for education...why bother? *Hands On!: Hands-on Math and Science Learning* (TERC) 21(2): 1-2, 23-24.

Samsel, R.W., G.A. Schmidt, J.B. Hall, L.D.H. Wood, S.G. Shroff, and P.T. Schumacker. 1994. Cardiovascular physiology teaching: Computer simulations vs. animal demonstrations. *Advances in Physiology Education* 11: S36-S46.

Sandquist, J. 1991. Student AVMA animal welfare committee survey on student surgeries. *Intervet* 25(1): 28-29.

Sapontzis, S. F. 1995. We should not allow dissection of animals. *Journal of Agricultural and Environmental Ethics* 8(2): 181-89.

Schmidt, K. 1999. Bill would allow students to say "no" to the knife. *Pioneer Press* (Barrington, Ill.), 4 March.

Schrock, J.R. 1990. Dissection. *The Kansas School Naturalist* 36(3): 3-16.

Schwartz, S., ed. 1992a. *Humane science projects manual: Grades pre-kindergarten through eight.* New York: United Federation of Teachers, Humane Education Committee.

———. 1992b. *Humane science projects manual: Grades pre-kindergarten through twelve.* New York: United Federation of Teachers, Humane Education Committee.

Self, D.J., A.B. Pierce, and J.A. Shadduck. 1994. A survey of the teaching of ethics in veterinary education. *Journal of the American Veterinary Medical Association* 204(6): 944-45.

Sewell, R.D.E., R.G. Stevens, and D.J.A. Lewis. 1995. Multimedia computer technology as a tool for teaching and assessment of biological science. *Journal of Biological Education* 29(1): 29-35.

Shapiro, K.J. 1987. A student's right to a careful education. *PsyETA Bulletin* (Fall): 9-11.

———. 1992. The psychology of dissection. *The Science Teacher* 59: 43.

———. 1998. *Animal models of human psychology: Critique of science, ethics and policy.* Seattle: Hogrefe and Huber Publishers.

Sieber, J.E. 1986. Students' and scientists' attitudes on animal research. *The American Biology Teacher* 48(2): 85-91.

Sinclair, M.J., J.W. Peifer, R. Haleblian, M.N. Luxenberg, K. Green, and D.S. Hull. 1995. Computer-simulated eye surgery: A novel teaching method for residents and practitioners. *Ophthalmology* 102: 517-21.

Smeak, D.D. 1998. Spotlight on a school: Ohio State University. *Alternatives in Veterinary Medical Education* 7: 4-5.

Smeak, D.D., M.L. Beck, C.A. Shaffer, and G. Gregg. 1991. Evaluation of video tape and a simulator for instruction of basic surgical skills. *Veterinary Surgery* 20(1): 30-36.

Smeak, D.D., L.N. Hill, M.L. Beck, C.A. Shaffer, and S.J. Birchard. 1994. Evaluation of an autotutorial-simulator program for instruction of hollow organ closure. *Veterinary Surgery* 23: 519-28.

Smith, W. 1990. Dissection and use of animals in schools. *The Australian Science Teachers Journal* 36(4): 46-49.

——— 1994. Use of animals and animal organs in schools: Practice and attitudes of teachers. *Journal of Biological Education* 28(2): 111-17.

Snyder, M.D., N.K. Hinton, J.F. Cornhill, and R.L. St. Pierre. 1992. Dissecting student objections: Responding to student concerns. *The Science Teacher* 59: 40-43.

Solot, D. 1995. The cultural meaning of middle school animal dissections: Frogs, fetal pigs, and the socialization of American youth. B.A. honors thesis, Brown University.

Solot, D., and A. Arluke. 1997. Learning the scientist's role: Animal dissection in middle school. *Journal of Contemporary Ethnography* 26(1): 28-54.

Souder, W. 1998. Evidence grows, suspects elusive in frogs' disappearance. *Washington Post,* 6 July, A3.

Stanford, W., W.E. Erkonen, M.D. Cassell, B.D. Moran, G. Easley, R.L. Carris, and M.A. Albanese. 1994. Evaluation of a computer-based program for teaching cardiac anatomy. *Investigative Radiology* 29(2): 248-52.

Stephanovsky, N. 1998. Human patient simulator enhances military medics' skills. *Military Medical Technology* (April-May): 22-23.

Stephens, M.L. 1986. *Alternatives to current uses of animals in research, safety testing, and education.* Washington, D.C.: HSUS.

———. 1987. The significance of alternative techniques in biomedical research: An analysis of Nobel prize awards. In *Advances in animal welfare science*, edited by M.W. Fox and L.D. Mickley. Boston: Martinus Nijhoff.

Stewart, M. 1989. The teaching of animal welfare to veterinary students. In *The status of animals*, edited by D. Paterson and M. Palmer. CAB International.

Strauss, R.T., and Kinzie, M.B. 1994. Student achievement and attitudes in a pilot study comparing an interactive videodisc simulation to conventional dissection. *The American Biology Teacher* 56(7): 398-402.

St. Remain, C. 1991. Cricket dissection. *outcast.gene.com/ae/AE/AEPC/-WWC/1991/cricket.htm.*

Stringfield, J.K. 1994. Using commercially available, microcomputer-based labs in the biology classroom. *The American Biology Teacher* 56(2): 106-8.

Stuart, D. 1988. Argentina bans dissection in schools. *Outrage* (December/January).

Takooshian, H. 1993. Lab animal controversy: Scientists versus the public? Paper presented at the April meeting of the Eastern Communication Association, New Haven, Connecticut.

Tauck, D.L. 1992. Teaching action potentials with computer simulations instead of neurons. *Humane Innovations and Alternatives* 6: 395-97.

Terry, T.M. 1992. Criticism of animal dissection impinges on academic freedom. *The Hartford Courant*, 21 July, D9.

Texley, J. 1996. Doing without dissection. *AV Magazine* 105(3): 10-13.

Teyler, T.J., and T.J. Voneida. 1992. Use of computer-assisted courseware in teaching neuroscience: the graphic brain. *American Journal of Physiology Advances in Physiology Education* 263: S37-S44.

Thanki, D. 1998. Virtual surgery in veterinary medicine. *AWIC Newsletter* 9(1-2): 11.

Thieme Interactive. n.d.. Virtual physiology: The unique truly interactive simulation software! Promotional brochure. *www.thieme.com.*

Townsend, P. 1985. Development of a dynamic model using the human placenta for microvascular research and practice. *Progress without Pain* (Spring): 6-8.

Tsang, S.M., M.J. Caluda, S.M. Steinberg, N.E. McSwain, L.M. Flint, and J.J. Ferrara. 1994. Laparoscopic cholecystectomy: What's so special? *Southern Medical Journal* 87:1076-82.

United Nations General Assembly. 1948. Universal Declaration of Human Rights, Resolution 217A (III), 10 December.

United States Department of Education. 1997. *The seven priorities of the U.S. Department of Education*, working document. *www.ed.gov/updates/7priorities/.*

USA Today. 1996. Around the nation: Wyoming. 9 September.

Van der Valk, J., D. Dewhurst, I. Hughes, J. Atkinson, J. Balcombe, H. Braun, K. Gabrielson, F. Gruber, J. Miles, J. Nab, J. Nardi, H. van Wilgenburg, U. Zinko, and J. Zurlo. 1999. Alternatives to the use of animals in higher education (ECVAM workshop report 33). *Alternatives to Laboratory Animals* 27: 39-52.

van Dongen, J.J., H.L. Bartels, J.W. Rensema, P.H. Robinson, and R. Remie. 1996. Training device for microsurgical anastomoses. *Animal Technology* 47(1): 19-27.

van Zutphen, L.M.F. 1989. Training programmes for biomedical scientists. In *Animal experimentation: Legislation and education*, edited by L.R.M. van Zutphen, H. Rozemond, and A.C. Beynen. Veterinary Public Health Inspectorate, Rijswijk. Utrecht, Netherlands: Department of Laboratory Animal Science.

van Zutphen, L.M.F, H. Rozemond, and A.C. Beynen, eds. 1989. *Animal experimentation: Legislation and education.* Veterinary Public Health Inspectorate, Rijswijk. Utrecht, Netherlands: Department of Laboratory Animal Science.

Vogt, R.C. 1981. Natural history of amphibians and reptiles in Wisconsin. Milwaukee, Wis.: Milwaukee Public Museum.

Walsh, R.J., and R.C. Bohn. 1990. Computer-assisted instructions: A role in teaching human gross anatomy. *Medical Education* 24(6): 499-506.

WARD'S. 1995. *WARD'S biology* (catalog) 1995. Rochester, N.Y.

Welch, L., and L. Luginbill. 1985. Dissecting and dining, or there's more than one way to slice a squid. *Science and Children:* 17-20.

Wenglinsky, H. 1998. *Does it compute?: The relationship between educational technology and student achievement in mathematics.* Princeton, N.J.: Educational Testing Service.

Wharton, D. 1996. Dissection of human corpse puts students to the test. *Los Angeles Times,* 22 May, B1.

Wheeler, A. 1993. Justifying the dissection of animals in biology teaching. *Australian Science Teachers' Journal* 36: 46-49.

White, K.K., L.G. Wheaton, and S.A. Greene. 1992. Curriculum change related to live animal use: A four-year surgical curriculum. *Journal of Veterinary Medical Education* 19: 6-10.

Willis, L.R., and H.R. Besch. 1994. Effect of experience on medical students' attitudes toward animal laboratories in pharmacology education. *Academic Physician and Scientist* (March): 11-13.

Wilmot, D., C. Safina, K. Hinman, D. Bolze, L. Speer, and M. Sutton. 1996. Comment letter to the U.S. Fish and Wildlife Service, Washington, D.C., 28 April. Ocean Wildlife Campaign.

Wolfe, M., N.D. Barnard, and S.M. McCaffrey. 1996. Animal laboratory exercises in medical school curricula. *Alternatives to Laboratory Animals* 24: 953-56.

World Society for the Protection of Animals (WSPA). 1994. Catching the cat thieves. *Animals International* (Summer/Autumn): 8-11.

————. n.d. *Investigation into the procurement of cats in Mexico for United States biological supply companies.* Boston: WSPA.

WSPA. *See* World Society for the Protection of Animals.

Young, J.A. 1984. Formaldehyde—the nose knows. *The Science Teacher* 51(6): 44.

Zierer, T. 1992. Cutting dissection in Ontario schools. Animals' Voice (Ontario SPCA) (Winter): 4-13.

Zinko, U., N. Jukes, and C. Gericke. 1997. *From guinea-pig to computer mouse: Alternative methods for a humane education.* Winchester, England: EuroNICHE, Sarsen Press.

Index

wavering on student choice, 72-73
National Research Council, 2, 5, 20
  standards of, 5
National Science Foundation, 4
National Science Teachers Association
  (NSTA), 2, 24
National Student Nurses Association
  support of conscientious objection,
  71
Nebraska Scientific, 31
Nobel Prize, 36
Norwegian Inventory of Audio-Visuals
  (NORINA)
  alternatives database, 47
nutritional deficiency studies
  problems with, 52
  The Great Grow Along, 52
Ohio State University, 40, 54, 58, 63,
  72
owl pellets, 7
Pancoast, Marian, 36-37
parents
  influence on students, 12, 14, 17
passive learning, 7
People for the Ethical Treatment of
  Animals (PETA)
  investigation of CBSC, 28-29
pharmacology
  use of alternatives for, 56-57
Physicians Committee for Responsible
  Medicine (PCRM) 57-58
physiology
  frog muscle labs, 53
  turtle heart labs, 53-54
  use of alternatives for, 55-56
pithing
  of frogs, 4, 19, 53-54
  of turtles, 53-54
plants
  as moral equals of animals, 38
  as subjects of study, 38

plastination, 7, 40
policies for student choice
  Chicago Public Schools, 74
  Connecticut, 74
  desirable elements of, 77-78
  Europe, 75-76
  Maryland, 74
  Massachusetts, 74
  Murdoch University, 76
  Sarah Lawrence College, 75
pound seizure, 30
Protect Our Earth's Treasures (POET),
  54
rabbits
  use of Freund's complete adjuvant in,
  54
Rana Laboratories, 27
rats
  embalming of, 28
  use in nutritional deficiency exercises,
  52
respect for life, 15, 39, 56
Rubaii, Safia, 74
Schrock, John Richard, 35-36
science fairs, 67
scientific literacy, 5-6, 17, 35
seal hunts
  children's attitudes towards, 17
Smithsonian Institution, 25
Solot, Dorian 13-15
sources of animals
  animal shelters, 30-31, 65
  biological supply companies, 26, 47
  deceased companion animals, 48
  ecological concerns regarding, 32-34
  farmed animals, 31-32, 47-48
  fur industry, 32
  naturally dead animals, 47-48
  student concern for, 10-12
  supermarkets, 24
  teacher explanation of, 13-14